OWN YOUR CAREER

GET UNSTUCK AND INTO A ROLE THAT SERVES YOU
- THE COMPLETE GUIDE TO CAREER
DEVELOPMENT, JOB SUCCESS, & PROFESSIONAL
FULFILLMENT: 2-IN-1 BOOK BUNDLE

DRAKE ELLIOTT

TABLE OF CONTENTS

THE CAREER OF CONSEQUENCE: FINDING WHAT SERVES YOU

UNSTUCK YOURSELF

THE CAREER OF CONSEQUENCE: FINDING WHAT SERVES YOU

INTRODUCTION

"Find out what you like doing best and get someone to pay you for doing it."

— KATHERINE WHITEHORN

Are you a new grad fresh out of school and looking for a job, perhaps saddled with student loan debt? Or maybe you are someone searching for purpose in your job and not finding it? Landing that "right" job is not as cut and dry as it used to be, especially as the marketplace has unprecedented change occurring within the interviewing process, which has become more challenging with the introduction of Artificial Intelligence.

Also, setting out on your own was once a rite of passage that was enjoyed by many young people, and now, it has become more difficult to become independent. Yet, there is hope for the soul searcher looking to start pursuing his or her goals in this global marketplace.

Are you ready to take the power in your life back into your own hands, starting with your career? Are you currently working at a job that sets your heart on your fire, or would you like to find it but don't know where to start? Then, look no further! Within this book you will find ways to overcome the interviewing obstacles that are standing in the way and preventing you getting ahead. With the case studies provided you can find your way. *I guess you've always wanted life on your own* (The Human League, 1984). Yes! You **can** live the life of your dreams and work in a career that will leave you truly fulfilled! After reading this book, you will know how to take the necessary steps to make a change.

This book is going to give you the knowledge of what steps you should take in order to move into the career of your dreams. You will experience ideological and philosophical expansion that will embolden you to put yourself in the right place at the right time, then ace the interviews that you must pass in order to climb to the top - fast!

I graduated from the Georgia Institute of Technology

with a degree in Engineering and Mathematics. A self-proclaimed nerd, I will admit that numbers have always fascinated me. Once I entered the workforce, I quickly realized that it is not an industry that is easy to advance in. I was eager to do more than just mathematics, so I climbed the ladder to success. I did a lot of introspection and realized where I landed did not serve my personal passions well, and I made a change. I learned that, just because you are good at something does not mean it is your calling or passion.

I am sharing my secrets with you in this book of self-discovery and a reclamation of ownership over your career life, whether you aim to climb the corporate ladder or pivot. This this book aims to help you find the career of consequence – the one that serves you where you are today.

As you go through the book, I encourage you to use this opportunity to reflect. Write it down as we go along to help you understand your trajectory. What's your next move? Where do you see yourself in one, two, or even five years from now? Think about the things you want to accomplish. Life is short, so you're not going to do something that doesn't give you purpose simply because of financial obligations alone, right? Life is a marathon, not a sprint, so finding a career you love is going to be an essential key to your overall happiness.

Think about what you can do when you take hold of your career – just imagine the possibilities, because they are endless! You can be the best *you* there is. Work a dream, leave a legacy.

Always start your days with gratitude, a positive and optimistic mindset, and remember that anything is possible. Believe that you deserve it and that the only one standing in your way is you. If you truly want and desire it, you *can* have it. Soak up the truths in this book and allow them to permeate as you discover how you can own your career, one that serves you, fulfills you, and makes you want to get out of bed happy to do it. But that's for you to create.

Go and Own it!

1

DO YOU OWN YOUR CAREER?

M any people, most people, are blindly performing tasks at a job and establishing a career that does not actually satisfy their personal desires. Too many people are just going through the motions, working jobs that their parents wanted them to pursue or that their society assured them was the "right move". They have the approval of their peers and so they stagnate, but deep down inside everyone knows that on some level they are not happy within this reality.

Are you looking for purpose but trying to find it in the desires of your parents? To be successful, earn a lot of money, and retire with millions of dollars - is that success? If you look to the desires of others and their expectations of you, then you will not be happy.

Instead, you will be miserable. It will make you into an ogre roaming the earth with constant feelings of malaise and a negative attitude. You will not find your manifest destiny. Rather, you will be looking to the interests of others and what they want for you. You will be living, not for **You** but for **Them**. Why do you allow that to happen?

Others will always build their expectations of us based on their assumptions and perceptions of us. They might judge us based on our appearances, so we try to make ourselves look good in front of others. We put on a lot of make-up, buy a lot of expensive clothes, invest in cars and luxurious homes, all because we want to *keep up with the Joneses*. Competition is always rife in these situations such that it ultimately takes away from our overall happiness and provides the seeds for the judgment of others.

Let me tell you something. The validation and approval of others *cannot* and *will not* make you happy. Becoming a slave to the acceptance of others is not the way to build your happiness and well-being on this earth. If you live by man's approval, you will die by man's approval, and no one cares how many people you pleased when you are on your deathbed.

Once you realize what makes you happy and how you can pursue that, then you can move past the suffering of seeking validation from others and work towards your own career so that you are fully in control. To begin this journey in what marks your career, let's begin with the basics of career building.

WHAT IS A "CAREER?"

The Oxford Dictionary has multiple definitions of what it means to have a career. Let's look at several of them.

- "An occupation undertaken for a significant period of a person's life and with opportunities for progress" (Lexico, Powered by Oxford).
- "The time spent by a person while committed to a particular profession" (Lexico, Powered by Oxford).
- "Working permanently in or committed to a particular profession" (Lexico, Powered by Oxford).

A broader understanding of one's career goes beyond just a job. Some people would stop and say that your career is your job, but there is much to this notion. It is important to understand that your career is something that you wish to pursue over a long-term commitment, it is just not a one- or two-year gig. Some companies might suggest that you are pursuing a career, when it's only a job. Search engines say that you're doing a "career search," when, in fact, it's only a job search that you're doing. When you're searching for a career, you're looking for something that is going to satisfy you for a long time. It is a job which continues past two, five, or even ten years and beyond.

Let's further point out the distinction between a career and a job. A career is a long-haul position that you are in for several years or even decades. A job is something that you use to build your resume and boost your chances of landing the job of your dreams. A job is also something that you work toward with a large invest-ment of training, education, and skills development because you need to find your way in this world. Careers take years of investment, and you don't want to choose the wrong one. Life is too short to waste on frivolous and mindless repetitive work that is not going to grant you the satisfaction you deserve. On the other hand, jobs are more transient. They connect to the overall concept of career; however, they are not an end in themselves.

A career gives you a sense of satisfaction that you derive from your work. If you find a career that you love, then you can keep pursuing your passions with complete happiness. With a growth mindset, you will feel the ability to succeed in all your endeavors, which will, in turn, make you excited about what you do. which makes going into work more of a fun task than a mundane chore that you do when you wake up to your alarm clock at 6 AM every day.

The negative points include the fact that you may feel unsatisfied in your job. If you choose unwisely, you might find yourself hating it and having no way around it. You won't be able to do the things you want to do, and you could end up despising your everyday tasks and only living for a paycheck and retirement account that will sustain you for twenty years when you're done working. Also, you might be living for those vacations that come only rarely during the year. But honestly, who wants to do that? If you're already counting the hours until your workday ends from the moment you start, then you must know you're in the wrong job – and certainly not in your career.

WHO CURRENTLY OWNS YOUR CAREER?

In this whole process, you need to be asking yourself the hard questions. Let's get straight to it: do you own your career or have you left it in the hands of your managers? Also, does your current job provide the fulfillment you're looking for? Are you in the position you dream of and wish to be in, or are you simply working to pay the bills every month?

A recent Gallup poll showed that 50% of Americans are not engaged with their work and 20% are actively disengaged. 51% of US workers feel that their work matters and that they identify with it (Vojinovic, 2019). 30% of American workers take a job just so they can pay their living expenses. Finally, 46% of American employees trust their employers (Vojinovic, 2019). There are many workers dissatisfied with their jobs these days. They work at a job that pays the bills, but they are left unsatisfied because they are disengaged at work. The work itself does not excite them or motivate them. Furthermore, many of them are just going to jobs so they can collect their pensions and simply retire after years of working at the same company with a steady paycheck. Yet, many American workers now place less trust in their employers than before, making them unhappy and less productive at work.

In most cases, workers will want to be supported by their superiors and guided in all the tasks they must do to perform their work. They will want trusted supervisors they can work with on projects and who can train them to help further their skills. Additionally, American workers want to have a company where they can be actively engaged in their work and not merely work as a cog in a machine. Many Americans are seeking this kind of job. And the American Dream of managerial positions has also become a motivating factor for

American workers, who want to climb the corporate ladder to bigger and better opportunities.

However, rank isn't the only deciding factor in what job American workers wish to pursue. 83% of millennial workers believe that work-life balance is the most important factor in evaluating a potential job (Gerke, 2015). With life-balance, millennials want a place where they can do their work and have a life on the side to do hobbies, sports, and other activities. These young people are investing their lives in things other than work and need to have time for their interests, family, and spouses, which enables them to be more productive at work. Therefore, it is crucial that millennials find work that suits their unique personalities.

Through taking back control of your career, you take back control of your life and of your happiness. This is the key aspect of how you can live a more meaningful and enjoyable life. You deserve to work in a satisfying career, so start working toward this goal today by determining which type of career best suits you.

KEY TAKEAWAYS

It is important to choose your job wisely and choose something that leads to not just employment but a career. Many people drift from one job to another without a concrete plan of what to do in the future. However, if you are mindful of what path you want to take, then you can succeed in attaining your dreams. It will be possible for you to do all the things on your list. Finding a career that suits you personally, professionally, and financially will be a big step that will help you take control of your life and lead a happier future. Discover a career that is right for you, one that will make you into the best person and professional that you can market to others.

2

YOUR CAREER SHOULD SERVE YOU

L et me share one important piece of wisdom with you: your career should serve you. Are you pursuing your dream, your vision, or someone else's? Our society teaches us to focus on our careers first and then to live. However, I think this is backward thinking. We should be living our lives first and then doing what we need to do in order to earn a living where we have space and time. Furthermore, our pursuits should fulfill us by tapping into our own personal values and core beliefs.

Looking at Google, you can find 1.4 million pages with articles, books, videos, training programs, and other things that focus on what it means to have a "great career" (Caprino, 2013). However, most of these resources only talk about the outer tactics that you need to use so you can succeed in your career but fail to discuss the inner happiness that you create for yourself through what you do.

You may think you know what it means to be successful based on your financial or social status. But all these things are attained in relation to other people. You might find fulfillment in your work, but you will be working toward earning other people's approval and you will feel empty while knowing you aren't being your best self.

WHAT DOES "HAVING A CAREER THAT SERVES YOU" ACTUALLY MEAN?

What does it mean to have a career that serves you? To put it simply, "having a career that serves you" leaves you feeling fulfilled. It makes you excited to go to work every day. You don't feel like your work is work. Instead, it's almost like play and it makes you want to jump up and down and do push-ups for several straight hours because it motivates you to keep doing the work you enjoy and want to do.

Moreover, you will feel yourself getting lost in work because you are so excited about it. Time will pass super quickly because you will be doing the job and not getting up from your desk or workspace until it's time to go. And that might be well past quitting time because you're so invested in the work you're doing. Working late is something you do because your passion calls you to get things done, so you stay in the office and accomplish the tasks that need to be completed because you want to check them off your to-do list. And you're determined to complete all your assignments in a timely and orderly fashion.

If your everyday work serves you, it will set you free. You'll no longer feel that you are enslaved by the expectations of others, and you'll be able to focus on what is important, which is your personal happiness. Find that there is a meaning and purpose to your life, and then pursue that with all the energy you have. Your career does not limit you; rather, it empowers and enables you to do things that will advance your personal goals and aspirations. You won't feel tied down to a particular place or job. You will find the opportunities that advance your personal mission statement and lead you to the Promised Land of opportunity, which may be working for Samsung, Mercedes, Apple, or even perhaps, yourself.

With a career that serves you, it all comes down to owning your career the way you want it to be. Do you live your life the way you wish, or do you only get to live as your career allows? The sooner you get to the point where you're taking control of the wheel of your career, the better your position will be and the happier you will feel. Owning your career is the best way to pursue that path, and I highly recommend you go in that direction for your future success, which is measured not in monetary gain or popularity but rather in personal fulfillment and meaning.

HOW CAN YOU FIND A CAREER THAT SERVES YOU?

What do you need in your career to lead a full and meaningful life? Here are some requirements your career must fulfill in order to be one that serves you and some actions you can take in order to find your dream career.

1. Healthy Boundaries

One of the most essential things you need in your life is strong boundaries, which help you to make sound and cogent decisions for your life. Often, you may let your guard down and allow people to trample on your boundaries, which, in turn, leaves you empty and help-less. When you try to please others and allow them to abuse or mistreat you, then you are setting yourself up for a life that will be empty and meaningless. What is a boundary? It is a barrier that you construct for yourself that guards you from outside influences on your life. When your boundaries are out of whack, you will find yourself unable to function and you will not be able to do the things you need to do. However, when your boundaries are too rigid, then you will not form lasting and meaningful connections with people in your life. Balance is key and will help you achieve your goals.

2. Financial Responsibility

In your career, you will not be able to be successful and happy if you allow money to be the primary motivation for your work. You might be motivated by money for a while, but eventually, it will suck your soul dry. However, if you understand what you need to be doing with your money and think about your values, then money will follow all your pursuits. Doors will open and opportunities will come to you. Instead of focusing on what your paycheck will look like, think about what you can do that will motivate you to do a job besides money. Reflect on how you want to live your life while serving your fellow man or woman and how you can contribute meaningfully to causes that matter in this world. If you base your decisions entirely on money, you will end up regretting it and ruin your career.

3. Think About Your Own Happiness

Psychologist Shawn Achor has said that if you can

access your inner happiness, you will set yourself up for success in all areas of life (Achor, 2011). Happiness leads to your success, not the reverse. Define what happiness means to you. It does not look the same for everyone. Some people can live on more or less money. People have different value systems and various aspects of life that make them different. Pursue your own version of happiness, not someone else's. Then, you will be truly happy.

4. Establish a Support System that Will Lead and Guide You

Building positive relationships with people is one of the most enriching and important things you can do. Often, you may find yourself getting carried away with your own personal vision of what your life and career should look like and become so self-driven and motivated that you don't look to the other people around you, who can give you a boost of energy and drive to do the things you always wanted to do. When you have a strong support system in place in your life, nothing can darken your world because you'll always know that there are people who care immensely about your success and will help you get there.

People who are most successful in their lives and careers tend to be people with a thankful heart. Take time to acknowledge the people who have made a difference in your life by showing your gratitude to your mentors. These are the people who guide you throughout your career and can be invaluable when it comes to finding your dream career. When you bring joy to others, you'll also feel that joy return back to you.

5. Get Away From People and Things that Take Away Your Energy

One of the biggest things that can take away your energy are the manipulators and toxic people in your life, who are often energy-sucking individuals who have no personality and don't contribute to building your career. Stay as far away from them as you can. People who are negative and toxic are not going to care about your success. Instead, they will only be intent on discouraging others from following their life path because their intent is the destruction of people's careers and livelihood.

Furthermore, there may be some activities and aspects of your schedule that drain energy from you. You should make every effort to avoid things that take away from your limited energy resources. For example, if you waste time and energy on fruitless things such as Netflix reruns and wasteful time on the Internet, you can find ways to minimize the time you spend on things that take away from your ability to pursue your dreams.

6. Face Your Fears and Anxieties

Lastly, it is important for you to be brave and face your anxiety and fear. Are you scared of making a career mistake? Are you afraid of what people think of you? Are you paralyzed by fear of disappointing yourself or other people? Then, you should realize that some of your fears may be imagined and you're worrying too much. Don't fear the return on investment on the things you love. Don't allow anxieties to overcome you. Instead, face the situations and people in your life and do the things that matter to you. Making your next career move will require your confidence and courage. The more you can muster up the strength to face the things that scare the crap out of you, the more you will be empowered to do the things that are going to advance your career.

What are you waiting for? The choice is yours. You have to own up to what you want in your career and where you want to be. Don't allow situations or other people to determine this for you. You must be responsible for yourself and do the necessary things to own your career.

CASE STUDY: RACHEL

Rachel thought that having a job with a high salary and benefits was going to be the best thing for her and that if she pursued a career in architecture or business, she would feel that her career fulfilled her. Having gone to architecture school, Rachel realized that she was not going to be happy with architecture for the rest of her life. She discovered that money could not buy happiness and that following something her parents had envisioned for her future was not going to satisfy her. Dismayed at the opportunity cost of wasting several years of her life and savings on an education that was not going to make her happy, Rachel knew that she had to make a change. She needed to do something that would.

One of the things she absolutely loved was zoo animals. She enjoyed going to the zoo, reading about the different endangered species, and finding animals that she could nurture and support. Rachel had taken some classes on zoology at her university, but she wanted to go even further with how involved she was with helping endangered animals. Rachel knew that she had a cause she believed in and, by doing work for the environment and community, she felt like her work was going to be important. While Rachel knew she would not be paid a huge salary, she was instead was inspired and fulfilled by the work itself. Rachel wanted to do work that was going to have meaning and significance for the world around her. She got her wish and was immensely satisfied with the work she did.

Key Takeaways

In summary, a career that serves you should be one that fits within the boundaries you set for your life and should fit your definition of happiness. In order to find such a career, you should be sure to establish a support system that is free from negativity and avoid allowing your fear to limit you. One thing you can start doing right now is to bullet journal on topics one through three. Think deeply about what matters most to you and write it down. You can do the same for topics four through six. List the individuals who've made the greatest impact on your career development, and if you feel that this list is lacking, then look for ways to expand your network. Don't worry though, we'll go over networking in depth later on. Finally, if you feel like fear is holding you back, think of one small way to challenge yourself every day or week until you've moved past your limitations.

3

TUNE IN TO YOUR PURPOSE

N ow, you might be wondering, *how can I get to a place where my career serves me as opposed to limits me?* This chapter will provide an answer to this question. We are now going to delve into what it is that drives you, your purpose, and how that plays into what your professional goals truly are.

HAVING A PURPOSE

Some people believe that you have a purpose in this life that needs to be fulfilled, while others think that it doesn't exist. But don't you want to make a living doing something that makes you feel alive and satisfied every single time you do it? Don't you want to feel happy and fulfilled? Don't you want to feel purposeful? Then, you must find something that gets you up in the morning. What is it that truly motivates you in your life? What is the *raison-d'etre* that brings you to where you are at this moment? That is what having a purpose is all about.

HOW DO I FIND MY PURPOSE?

Now that you know what it is like to have a purpose, you can discover how you can find this seemingly elusive "purpose." Think about your interests. What are your hobbies? Maybe you like to run laps across a track. Maybe you like to volunteer at the local animal shelter where you help animals who have been endangered by external circumstances. Perhaps, you might be a volunteer at a nursing home, aiding older adults in their everyday mundane tasks. Or, you might be a lifeguard at the local pool and enjoy swimming in your free time. Also, it might be possible you enjoy plucking your guitar or playing the piano in your free time, but you're not sure what to do with the hobby.

You likely have a hobby or hobbies that you could turn into a career if you wanted to do that. But you may be too scared to do the things that truly give you passion because you are afraid of not being able to support yourself doing them. You are fearful that if you pursue your true passions that you won't get paid enough to live the life you want to live. So, you simply allow yourself to do your hobbies on the side, make a lot of money with your 9-5 desk job, and think that things are suddenly going to get better for you later.

Hobbies can contribute to your financial well-being. They don't have to be something that you simply put on your to-do list after your work hours. You can make them part of your daily life, and they can also be monetized because you can pursue a successful side hustle that could eventually evolve into your own business. You never know. There are successful writers and artists who started out with their side hustle alongside their 9-5 job that only paid the bills. Within months or years, they were able to start a new career and work full-time on the things that gave them passion.

1. *What Makes You the Happiest?*

Now, think about something that gives you joy, more than anything else in your life. Perhaps, it is your dog or cat. Maybe, it is that guitar that you love to play when the going gets tough. Or, perhaps, you really like painting or sculpting in your spare time and that gives you a lot of happiness. Think about the things that make you most joyful and alive and consider those things that contribute to your personal fulfillment. This will help you think about your purpose and how you can accomplish it.

If we're honest with ourselves, there are a lot of things in our lives that detract from our overall happiness. Much of our mundane lives, including everyday tasks at our 9-5, contribute to our stress and anxiety and not to our happiness. Do you want to continue doing the things that are not giving you happiness but are taking away from it? Do you want to continue to slave away at a job that only pays you a modest salary and will not give you the lifestyle you deserve? Think about such things.

2. *Where Do You Find the Most Peace?*

Next, you should think about the place and activities that give you the most peace. Perhaps, that is sitting working on your next book project or a painting project in your studio. Maybe, that is hitting the gym and doing your daily routine. Or, you might feel most at peace when you're simply with your friends talking at a cafe and having a nice cup of tea or coffee.

Consider the people, places, and activities that give you the greatest sense of peace. Do you like to be around positive, upbeat, and hardworking people who encourage you to pursue your dreams and accomplish your goals? Or, do you like to be in places that promote productivity, innovation, and exploration? Do you want to do activities that inspire and energize rather than drain and discourage you?

Think about the aspects of your life that are giving you peace. When you are in those situations, you will find that you're in an effortless space. Everything falls into place perfectly, and you don't have to worry about things the way you used to; instead, you feel that your life is going in the right direction. People and opportunities come your way as if by accident, but it is totally intentional. Call it destiny, if you will.

3. *A Technique to Find Your Purpose: Use a Venn Diagram*

One way that you can find your purpose is by using a Venn diagram. This method was clearly explained by Clark Kegly, who is a life coach (Clark Kegley-Refusing to Settle, 2016). He demonstrated how to find it. Consider making your own Venn Diagram of the three categories described below.

a) Credibility

Draw a circle to show what you're credible in, if that is technology, teaching, coaching, whatever it may be. Your area of credibility is ideally something that you have spent the last 5-10 years doing, which would make you an expert in this domain. Choose a niche or topic that you have been working on for a while now. Maybe you've gotten a Ph.D. or finished a five-year stint teaching English in Japan.

Think of the topics that you have become an expert on and could easily educate and inform others about. What would your friends say about you? Would they say that you're an expert on trading or marketing? Look at the recommendations you have received on LinkedIn. What do they say about your credibility in the field that you have been working in for a while? By answering these questions, you will be one step closer to discovering your purpose.

b) Saturday Night

Now, think about what you might be doing on a Saturday night. Maybe you're watching the football team on your TV or the latest Netflix rerun. Perhaps, you enjoy hiking, so you're outside soaking in the sunlight while working up a sweat on the trail. Or, maybe you like to go to the gym so you can prove yourself to the other men and women with your six-pack abs. Think about the daily activities that give you passion and how you can use those toward your purpose.

Next, look at your credit card statements and see where all your money is going. Look at PayPal and browse your online statements. Where are you spending your money? It is crucial for you to know where your priorities are and what things you're willing to pay for because that will be the next key to unlocking the secret of what could be the best career move for you.

Consider the things that you're most comfortable talking about, which give you a sense of meaning and drive that will take you where you want to go.

c) Demand

Now that you've considered what you're credible at and what would be your favorite topic to talk about on a Saturday night, you can think about the demand and where you can use your talents and interests for your personal mission. Finding a demand for your niche is going to be a key way you can monetize your gifts and talents because you will know that people desire what you have to offer and are willing to pay you money for these goods and services. The key element is filling a demand rather than creating a demand. It is a lot easier to find a need that needs to be filled rather than try to create one out of your own desire to advance your career. Think about what the world needs at this time. What is the most pressing need that people in your field have and are willing to pay someone for?

With your newly discovered item that needs to be completed, you can find a business model to follow in the niche or trade that you'd like to work in. This will allow you to get a feel for what it is like in the field and will give you the experience necessary to emulate the people you're trying to be like. Find two or three people who could be role models for you that you can seek to become like and then follow suit with what they're doing.

Having chosen the models you seek to emulate, you can now focus on using search engines and resources that will help you to train yourself and develop your skills and expertise, which will lead you to your passion and desired field. It will help to combine all these aspects together.

Your Purpose: The Intersection

Looking at the Venn Diagram, you can see that the intersection of your credibility, Saturday night topic, and demand will be your purpose. As you bring together all these aspects, you can find your purpose and do what you were meant to be doing all along. This is not a scientific formula, but rather, it is a helpful tool that will help you brainstorm what your purpose is and find what you should be doing with your life. It is incredibly useful and will enable you to lead a fantastic career.

FIVE TOOLS TO FIND YOUR PURPOSE

Aside from this Venn Diagram, there are numerous other ways to find your purpose. You can begin by asking yourself different series of questions, which will lead you to find the answer. Let's begin with the first question.

1. Who are your heroes?

Think about the people that you look up to and hold in high regard. Do they have several things in common? For teachers, they often have teachers that they look up to, because they seek to emulate the aspects of their lives that they greatly respected when they were their teachers' students. Consider the people you respect and start looking at the things that you have in common with those people. When you examine this question, you will find some clues as to what your purpose is, because you will hold the people who are your heroes in high esteem (Perception Trainers, 2014).

2. What do people come to you for the most?

There are some things that we do naturally that make us a natural asset. People will come to us when they have a question about a topic because we are deemed knowledgeable or capable of handling a given situation. For example, let's say that you are a person that your friend always calls when caught in a bind or in trouble, and you help them out or give them moral support. Or, perhaps, someone will consult you about the latest techno-gadgets on the market because you have some expertise in this area. When you are living out your purpose, you will feel that there is a sense of ease with what you are doing because you are exercising your natural gifts and talents.

3. What would you do if you never had to work another day in your life?

Imagine that you have won the lottery and have 20 million dollars. You must do something on a deserted luxurious island, where you want to retire at age 40. You don't have to hold down a job to pay the bills. Everything is already taken care of for you. But at this point, you will want to keep yourself busy with a task that is not job-related. Think about the things that bring you joy that you don't need to use to earn money and consider how you can use those for your purpose. When you do this, you will find that you can discover what your purpose is and use it as a guideline for all the different tasks you want to do (Perception Trainers, 2014).

4. What do you so easily take for granted?

Consider the things that you don't easily think about,

that are necessities in your life. They might be relationships, your computer, savings account, or other matters. What are the things that you're neglecting to put energy into because you're so busy? Think about this matter and what you can do with that. If you think about your necessities and desires, then you will find what is truly important to you, and you won't neglect them. These crucial aspects of your life will keep you going and help you accomplish all the things you want to in your life.

5. What are the things you treasured as a child?

Now, think about the things you used to treasure as a child. Did you enjoy playing school with your younger brothers or sisters? Did you enjoy playing the piano or violin at a recital? Did you relish going out and dancing with your friends to the Macarena? What were some of the things you valued? When you see what you liked as a child, you can get a glimpse of what your career will look like later. Childhood dreams and aspirations can be the fuel to your future ambitions and can shine a light on what you truly want in your life. When you were a child, your heart and soul yearned for something that you could not put a finger on at the time. Right now is the time to tap into that soul urge and discover what it is that you're truly meant to do based on the information that you gather from your past experience and childhood.

OTHER WAYS TO DISCOVER YOUR PURPOSE AND TRUE MEANING

As you can see, asking yourself probing self-reflective questions is an important method for uncovering the depth of your heart's true desires. And this is an essential way to lead you to discover your purpose. However, you can dig deeper into that by cultivating important habits, which will enable you to find your purpose. Let's look at some habits you can pick up today to find your significance in this world.

1. Read, as Much as Possible

Reading is a window into the world. It is a central way to discover the truth and meaning in society, and literacy is an important part of providing you with purpose in your life. The more you read, the more in tune with your surroundings you become. Educating yourself through the reading of articles, books, monographs, and online resources enables you to become a thinking being, who actively questions the world around you. It is vital for you to find ways you can engage with others through this medium of reading.

Digital literacy is an important buzzword in modern

times because an increasing proportion of reading materials now comes from online resources. Literacy is no longer limited to simply books in a library. More than ever, society is turning its focus to the Internet, which is a goldmine of resources that enables you to advance literacy and encourages you to read many things.

Because literacy is a crucial aspect of your development, I highly recommend that you read as widely as possible. Find a news article, read an interview, browse an advice column, and by whatever means possible, read about something that interests you. You don't have to be stuck behind some stuffy old book in a library. Discover the topics that give you energy and read up on them. Become an expert on your passions by reading widely and finding other resources to improve your skills in these areas.

There are a variety of resources you can find on topics online, including National Geographic, the New York Times, BBC, among others. Educational organizations around the world have made their content available online, which allows you to find reading material that energizes and motivates you to read (Smith, 2018).

2. Find Community That Supports You in Your Endeavors

One of the most important parts of finding your purpose is finding common ground with others who share the same views and interests. Community is a crucial aspect in finding your purpose. You need to have a strong community of like-minded people who can support you in your efforts to develop your skills and talents. Many people find a community in religious circles or churches. Others join volunteer organizations that cater to their values. It is important to find an organization that you want to contribute to and offer the skills and expertise that you have, which can make a difference in this world. Often, when you find a company or organization that matches your values, skills, and other attributes, you will find purpose and meaning, as well as a career that will sustain you for the long run.

3. Cultivate Feelings of Awe, Altruism, and Gratitude

One important thing that can give you joy in your life is when you can have feelings of awe for something that is greater than you. Whenever you express your wonder at the world around you, you become emotionally wired for a purpose that is beyond yourself, not just limited to your quiet little corner of the world, and it motivates you to do things for others. You come to realize that people are sick, poor, and dying out there, and you need to have a personal mission to aid others in need.

This sense of awe leads you to altruistic efforts, in which you choose to help others out of the generosity and alacrity of your heart. So, you walk a lady with her groceries to her car and help her get in. You go build a house for someone who is in need. You serve soup at a soup kitchen because you want to feed the hungry. Or, you volunteer at a homeless shelter and seek the welfare of those who have no refuge or place to put their head at night. When you look outside of yourself to a mission that is beyond you, you realize how much the world needs people who are caring, in awe and wonder, and altruistic, who can be world changers. You can make a difference in this broken world and provide joy to those who need it.

Furthermore, your altruism leads you to express gratitude for what you have received. When you feel thankful, you are a lot happier as a person. Unlike the people who tend to complain, you feel grateful for the opportunities that have come your way and don't feel you simply deserved them or were entitled to them. Instead, you recognize that every day is a gift of grace from above and that you cannot explain it. But you just want to live each day as it comes and do your best to live a meaningful and purpose-driven life (Smith, 2018).

4. Telling Your Story

One of the most powerful ways of teaching and leading people to believe in a cause is through testimony. Within religious circles, testimony-sharing is one of the best ways to witness to others about your faith. In the same way, how you share your story invites people to see where you are in the universal story of human history. You connect people to common themes and ideas in your story that are joined with the themes of humanity. The brotherhood of man allows you to empathize with those who are struggling and enables you to be there for others. When you connect with the stories of others and they with yours, there is a tie that binds you together that speaks to your soul and allows you to experience healing. Sharing your story is going to be one of the most valuable ways you can contribute to society, and it will give you a greater sense of purpose than ever before. Find a platform where you can tell your story, whether that is through writing it out on a blog or sharing a vlog or video clip with your friends and family. It will be a powerful tool to help shape the world around you and give you a greater sense of purpose (Smith, 2018).

HOW TO ALIGN YOUR MISSION WITH YOUR NEWFOUND PURPOSE

Your mission in life is not to achieve fame and success, contrary to what the American Dream states. It is not your mission to achieve riches and glory on this earth, for all of those things pass away in a blink of an eye. Material riches are not going to last. Even money is not going to keep you going for a long time. You could have all the money in the world and still be a miserable, sorry old person without a friend who can share in your troubles.

No, instead, you should see the fact that there is so much more to our world than money, power, and fame. All those things have corrupted human beings since the beginning of humanity, and they will cause you anxiety, fear, and depression, if you are privileged to attain them. Think of all the Hollywood stars, who despite earning millions of dollars and having numerous adoring fans, have eating disorders, are suicidal, are clinically depressed, and are just plain miserable. You would be astounded to see the facts and figures for that issue. It is simply insane.

Rather than focusing on all the things the American Dream is trying to lure you into, you should focus on your inner heartbeat. What is it that keeps you going?

What enables you to burn the midnight oil? What cause do you believe in, that you think will make a difference in this broken, miserable world? Consider your personal mission statement and what that means for your life. It will change your life. It is important for you to move past your own selfish desires and think about a purpose that is going to take you outside of thinking so much about just yourself, to thinking more about what *you* can do for *others*. Think about the kind of impact you want to make on this world and choose a career that is going to work according to that purpose.

Too many people in America are focused on attaining their American Dream, selfishly and vainly pursuing something that is not meant to last. But you should think differently. Be thoughtful about what you can do to change the world. Start with having a mindset and purpose which will shape the way you interact and engage with others in society. Are you giving back to the world around you? Think about what you can do for your fellows in a world that needs people who are empathetic, kind, caring, gentle, and peaceful. Make a difference in the community where you live or extend your global reach to impact impoverished regions.

KEY TAKEAWAYS

Having considered your purpose, you're ready to take control of your career. Allow yourself to be centered on your purpose. Don't forget your center. It's going to be the compass that leads you to the green pastures of this world. Aligning yourself with your purpose will be a crucial turning point as you decide what you want to do with your life. And it's never too late to start thinking about it. Maybe you're in your 20s or 30s and still don't have life figured out. Well, that's okay, you don't have to. Take it easy and consider what you can do right now to contribute to the world around you. By living your life with a career that has meaning and purpose and an altruistic spirit, you will enable yourself to be not just a career man or woman but a world changer.

4

DEVELOP YOUR PEOPLE SKILLS

The primary intention of this chapter is to discuss the power that coincides with having positively oriented social capabilities. In business, the hands-down number one advantage any person has is their connections. Connections come as the byproduct of one's capacity for networking. This chapter will deep dive into the essence of what positive people skills look like in the workforce, how one can use them to their advantage, and how even the most introverted individual can train and enhance their ability to socialize and promote themselves through networking.

PEOPLE TO PEOPLE: INTERPERSONAL SKILLS ARE VITAL

Having well developed interpersonal skills is incredibly important, especially as our world becomes more automated and machine learning impacts the workforce. There's a high priority for having employees who are able to communicate effectively and who can adapt to environments with diverse cultures. Let's look at some crucial people skills you will need to develop to improve your career success:

Having considered the rationale behind having good people skills, we can now look at what positive social skills can contribute to your life as a career man or woman. What does having positive social skills look like realistically?

1. Respect for Others

Respect is an important part of professional relationships and is an important part of job satisfaction. However, not all workplaces are places where people respect others. Instead, managers may berate their employees and people might be rivals against one another, which creates hostility and jealousy. These aspects can contribute to a negative work environment that is toxic for everyone involved. Therefore, it is crucial to develop respect for others in order to have a desirable workspace. This includes the following:

- Expressing gratitude and courtesy towards others
- Listening intently to what others have to say
- Respecting others' ideas and opinions
- Not insulting or attacking others for their difference of opinion
- Not taking credit for another's work even if you improved or built on their work (Big Think Edge, 2018)

2. Showing Empathy and Emotional Intelligence

Empathy and emotional intelligence are becoming an important part of everyday work life because in today's climate, you need to know how to relate to others and where they're coming from. This includes relating to the feelings and thoughts of other people around you. It helps you to be mindful of others and sensitive to their needs and desires, while communicating effectively. Professionals can develop and grow in this area by building empathy, which includes active listening skills.

3. Awareness of Nonverbal Cues

Nonverbal messages are an often overlooked aspect of our lives, but they help build a rapport with others around you, including your colleagues, partners, customers, and supervisors. Different forms of nonverbal communication include facial expressions, body language, gestures, eye contact, and physical contact, which includes shaking hands.

Much of what we communicate is actually not through our words but how we use our body language and other nonverbal cues, and it is important to be mindful of how we use them because that can make a pivotal difference in how we relate to others around us.

4. Showing Self-Awareness

Self-awareness is one aspect of emotional intelligence, and it is consciously being aware of your own emotions and thoughts. It is important for you to be self-aware so you can understand how you are being perceived by others around you, whether through your words or nonverbal cues that you are sending to others. It can either contribute to or detract from your success in your company (Big Think Edge, 2018).

5. Clear Communication

Direct communication is a crucial part of your personal and professional life. Therefore, being a good communicator is going to be the difference between success and failure in your career and life. Poor communication will lead to job dissatisfaction, unmet expectations, and could potentially cost you your job. Therefore, you should find ways to become an excellent communicator in both written and verbal form.

6. Proper Conduct

It is crucial for you to behave properly at work. What's appropriate at work can vary from place to place. However, there are certain universally recognized behaviors that you would do well to follow when you go into work.

- Be kind and respectful toward others
- Show politeness to your colleagues and managers
- Be on time
- Cooperate and don't complain
- Have a positive attitude
- Follow the dress code
- Be responsible for your own actions

7. Openness to Feedback

In order to grow professionally and personally, it is necessary to receive feedback on what we do. There is also a difference between feedback and criticism. Feedback can resemble criticism, but it is constructive and considers both the merits and drawbacks of a given situation or work performance of an individual. The objective of feedback is to give corrective advice that includes evaluation of a worker's performance; however, it is meant to help him or her in future work responsibilities and functions (Big Think Edge, 2018).

Criticism, on the other hand, only provides a judgment on the performance criteria, which can also be positive or negative, depending on the situation.

It is important to be open to feedback. It will allow you to grow and learn from others in your workplace. If you are not open to feedback, then you will likely stagnate or regress in your work life, which will not lead you to advance your career. Be positive and focus on the areas of your life that you can improve (Big Think Edge, 2018).

NETWORKING

One of the most important aspects of interpersonal skills is networking. This term refers to the exchange of ideas and information among people who have the same career or interests, and it usually happens in an informal social atmosphere.

Networking is the way that professionals form ties and contacts with people who are in their circles, discover new career opportunities in their field, and become informed about the news and developments in their respective fields or in society as a whole. Networking usually begins as a point of contact between people who didn't previously know one another (Kagan, 2019). Individuals share a common interest or professional affiliation, which brings them together in one place. Effective networking opportunities include a church or religious group, club, or a university alumni association.

For people in a workplace situation, networking occurs at professional seminars, conferences, and other events which cater to the interests of like-minded people.

There are different ways you can do networking, one of them is business networking, which takes place between business owners, and this type usually happens at local conferences and events. Business networking allows business owners to gain additional clients and opportunities that might not have been available to them before.

The other type is online networking, which takes place on online professional networking platforms, like LinkedIn. This platform is a professional social media network that connects employers and prospective employees, as well as other professionals. It also allows people the chance to post their resumes on a platform that can be easily browsed by employers to identify potential employees (Kagan, 2019).

Another part of people skills that is vital to networking is investing in social capital, which is the product of social interaction (Kenton, 2019). This includes the personal relationships that are developed between people in an organization that help promote trust and support, which leads to improved business performance. People in an organization work together toward a common goal. Social capital may also be compared with financial capital, which refers to the financial resources of a company. However, it might be considered just as valuable because it is the fruit of personal relationships between people who form connections that can last a whole career. Practically, about 85% of jobs are filled as a result of professional networking, which is the product of social capital (Kenton, 2019).

How does this benefit your business? It does so tremendously, in a variety of ways. When you have strong social capital, more people will be willing to invest in your company. You will have more applicants for your jobs and be able to hire people who desire to be part of your team. Additionally, you will be in the position to hire the best and the brightest to be members of your organization.

HOW YOU CAN USE YOUR PEOPLE SKILLS TO GAIN AN ADVANTAGE IN THE MARKETPLACE

Being easy to talk to is an important characteristic that will set you apart from the sea of applicants and working professionals. When you have excellent people skills, you will be more relatable and likable. When people have a problem or issue, they will come to you for support and advice. You will also build trust among the people in your group. Additionally, you will be able to snag the next job offer, because your future employer will instantly connect with you. Additionally, if you are confident and exhibit a sense of self-awareness, that will also draw people to you.

CASE STUDY: MINSEOK AND ALEX

Minseok was working on a project for a big tech start-up company in Seoul, South Korea. He had a problem that he wanted to solve, but he couldn't do it alone. There were computer issues and glitches that were causing problems for almost everyone in his company, and people were becoming agitated and unable to work for a while. Realizing that he had something he could contribute, including some knowledge of computer hardware, he collaborated with one of his team members, Alex. The two men worked together to solve the issue. They knew that two heads were better than one. They both got along well with one another and supported each other through the time of crisis.

Instead of panicking along with the rest, they came up with a solution together. And then, they assisted others in the office by going individually to each team member's computer to fix the problem. Instantly, Minseok and Alex became very popular in the office, and people raved about their personality because they were kind, generous, and helpful. This was the type of person you would want to be around in the office. Eventually, the company was able to solve the issue, and because of the kindness and ingenuity of both Minseok and Alex, everything went smoothly. Relationship building is an important part of work environments today, and whenever people collaborate on projects and provide unique solutions, companies are better for it and become more productive places to work.

CASE STUDY: ALLISON

Allison was a hardworking young lady who had just joined the Education First company. She was apprehensive at first because it was her first job out of college, and it was a big career move for her, as she had to move across the country from California to Boston, which was a significant relocation for her. Having to uproot herself was a challenge that she had to face. She would have to make new friends, form a new community, and integrate into her new workplace. With all the demands of moving, including finding an apartment, Allison had to adjust to her new surroundings in Boston. As she started her new job, Allison was able to quickly establish a rapport with her colleagues.

Instead of remaining intensively focused on her own work, she tried to get to know her colleagues and supervisors and asked them many questions to aid in getting started and taking on all her responsibilities. She also sought out the mentorship of a senior worker, who could help her manage her tasks and learn the tricks of the trade, which would help her integrate faster. During her lunch break and coffee time, she spent time getting to know people and did not keep to herself. Over time, she formed long-lasting relationships with people, and she was likable and friendly toward everyone she met. Allison was conscious of the kinds of communication she was using, including her nonverbal cues, and she was mindful of all her conduct so she would be respected by others. Because of her strong interpersonal skills, her supervisor became aware of the good work she was doing, and within a month, she was promoted to a new position, which had more responsibilities and even a higher pay scale. Allison was thankful that she was able to begin her climb up the ladder of success, and she owed it to her people skills, which were invaluable in building her career.

TOOLS AND TECHNIQUES FOR BUILDING YOUR PEOPLE SKILLS

With the given examples, you can see that people skills will grow your earning potential, as well as your ability to succeed in a company. You may be wondering, "How can I grow my people skills, so I can have what Minseok, Alex, and Allison have?" Well, here are some steps you can follow so you can be a socialite who is likable and dependable at your company.

1. Wear a Wardrobe Staple That Represents You

Do you wear orange shoes and a jacket? Do you wear that tweed coat? Or, maybe you wear those stiletto heels that everyone can hear coming around the corner? Maybe you also wear a purple shirt that represents a winner. Whatever you like to wear, you should wear something that represents you and that you can market to others. All of us have our unique personalities that are usually shown through what we wear. There is a lot you can tell about someone by what clothes they wear on an everyday basis. Are you wearing a suit and do you look trim every day? Or, are you into business casual? Find something that suits your unique style and show that to others. You will immediately stand out and you will display to the world around you your personal brand and style, which can be a powerful force in today's workspaces.

2. Become the Master of Smalltalk

Do conversations with strangers exhaust you? Do you find yourself having trouble relating to others? Think of everyday topics that people are talking about and try to weigh in on your own opinions of them. But one of the key aspects of small talk is not just knowing what to talk about. It is also what kinds of questions you can ask others, which shows your interest in them. Ask people personal questions that probe into their deep interests. For example, you could ask them, "What is something that really excites you whenever you go to work?" The more you do this, the more authentic and relatable you will seem because you don't want to just get to know people on the surface. You want to know what makes people tick and motivates them in their work.

3. Make Sure Your Online Profile Is the Real You

Often, in today's world, we like to sugarcoat our lives, especially with our online presence. We only want to show the glittery, Instagram-infused selves that are polished and better-than-real-life because we don't want to show our authentic side. Instead, we want to make others envy our lives because it makes us feel better. Rather than trying to make a name for yourself on social media, show your edgy and sometimes rough side. Show your vulnerabilities and make yourself more relatable. This authenticity builds trust and invites people into your space because they don't have to put you on a pedestal. They see that they can talk to you and can come into contact with you.

4. Create a Persuasive Narrative

An important part of selling something, including yourself, is through creating your own personal narrative. Everyone has a story to tell about their life, and stories speak to people's hearts and minds. There is a reason why testimony-sharing is so effective. When you have a persuasive story to tell others, they will see your authentic self and relate to your struggles, triumphs, and other aspects of your life. They will see the humanity in you that shows a story of overcoming adversity and allowing yourself to face the challenges of this hard life with grace and truth. Having a narrative is going to go a long way, and it could very well snag you the next big job opportunity.

5. Set the Mood

We tend to mirror the mood of the people around us. When someone in the room is in a bad mood, then we might feel the same way. But if you can cheer people up with your positive, can-do attitude, then others will feel the contagious positive energy, which will perk them right up. Setting the mood is a powerful tool that you can do whenever you want to fight the negativity in the room, including the chronic complainers who have nothing good to say on a given day. Having a good attitude is an important part of developing your social skills, which will, in turn, make more people want to spend time around you. Instantly, you will become likable and a lot of fun to be around.

6. Have a Helpful Demeanor

If you have a helpful spirit about you, then you will likely be a popular person in the office. Offering assistance to your new colleague? Resolving conflict when it arises between colleagues? These are all ways you can contribute to your office environment in by encouraging and supporting the people around you, and it will build your career and help your relationships with those in your workplace.

7. Be Unoriginal

Most of our best ideas have already been quoted somewhere in writing. Unfortunately, original ideas are hard to come by, unless you are a Shakespeare of today. However, that doesn't mean you can't be creative. You can be unoriginal and still contribute meaningfully to your environment. You only need to do well to attribute credit where it is due to the sources that inspire you. Liberally quote your favorite authors, entrepreneurs, and other people who have been helping you get your creative juices flowing. It shows honesty and integrity, which are necessary ingredients for a successful career.

8. Send Thank-You Notes to People Who Are Important to You

Lastly, it is important for us to show gratitude to people who are important to us. That includes thank-you notes and gifts that are a token of our appreciation to them. It goes very far in today's world, where a thankful heart is taken for granted. But people feel very good when they interact with someone who expresses thanks to others, as this gratitude symbolizes a lack of entitlement to the things they have received. Instead, they graciously receive help from someone important to you.

How Introverts Can Engage in Relationships and Develop People Skills

Now, there may be people in the room who are introverts, who shy away from engaging with people. Half of the world's population consists of introverts, and the workplace, unfortunately, has become a place that does not cater to them in ways that are damaging to their personality. We should never feel that it is our place to fix introverts and their unique way of viewing the world. Instead, we need to help them find ways to engage with others and come out of their shells into the workplace, where they can thrive and form meaningful relationships. Here are some ways they can do that.

1. Form Relationships With One or Two Colleagues

Introverts thrive on deep and meaningful relationships, but they only have the energy and space for a few people in their lives. They don't need to be the life of the party, and they don't need to be the most popular person in the room. Instead, they want to be understood, and often, that means they only need to relate to a few people in their circle. But once the trust has been made, introverts can be lifelong contacts and truly loyal people, who will get the job done. By allowing introverts to be paired with one or two people, they can thrive in an office environment and accomplish a lot. Sometimes, that also includes mentoring and other one-on-one relationships. Giving introverts the space to form a good relationship with a few colleagues will be an important step in integrating them into a company.

2. Give Them Time to Think

Especially in meeting settings, introverts tend to not express their thoughts freely in an open sharing format if they have not had the time to sit and think. Instead, they may be passive and only want to listen to others. However, if you give them time to think about the things they need to say, they will be able to open up and share what's on their mind and contribute meaning-fully to an office environment. By providing the agenda and other topics in advance, introverts can engage in discussions and offer their perspectives in a more relaxed and serene way, which makes them feel valued and trusted.

3. Allow Them to Do What They Do Best: Listening

An important part of being an introvert is being a good listener, and this always involves asking good questions. Introverts are curious people, and they will ask many questions. Their inquisitive nature makes them good conversationalists, and although they might not talk a lot with others around them, they can get others to talk for them and listen carefully. They will always offer a piece of advice and knowledge that someone has never thought of before. Allowing an introvert to listen to others will make their people skills increase substantially because others will value their input, as well as their counseling demeanor.

4. Work Independently and in a Small Group

Introverts are, by their nature, quiet workers, and they don't like to be seen when they are doing their work. Often, they will hide behind their cubicles or work from home, because that is where they do their best work. Introverts need to be uninterrupted because they cannot handle a lot of background noise. Therefore, they need space to think and reflect. This necessitates an office space that is quiet and has few distractions. Otherwise, introverts will struggle to get things done in a timely manner.

After introverts are done reflecting and thinking, they can contribute to small group discussions with no more than three or four people. Because introverts can get a lot done by themselves, they don't need someone to constantly check up on them. And once their work is done, they can share their unique ideas with others. By having periodic meetings, they can give updates on their progress and help others along the way. This, in turn, increases their social skills and makes them valuable players in their company.

5. Don't Make Introverts Do Small Talk

Small talk is one of an introvert's least favorite things to do because it is draining and sucks all the energy from their reserves. Introverts become easily exhausted at networking events, where they have to simply go with the flow and engage in small talk, although their introverted self wants to just go home and read a book. Introverts want to avoid small talk like the plague, so find some interesting topics to discuss, including the news, psychology, or other meaningful topics that speak to us all. You will have introverts talking in no time and connecting with others.

6. Communicate in Writing or Email

Introverts are naturally solitary people, and they often struggle to come up with the right words to say. Because of their quiet demeanor, they prefer to send text messages, write emails, and send other written forms of communication. Introverts often feel that they express their ideas best through writing, which is why they are some of the best writers in the world. Giving introverts the chance to write things down will help them be clear communicators, and they will easily thrive in a corporate setting if they can tap into this important skill.

7. Prepare Topics in Advance

Introverts thrive off advanced preparation and can

actively engage in conversations that they know a lot about. If you have an agenda or different topics you want to address, give the introverts in your company a heads up. It will make them feel a lot more comfortable and able to interact with others. Because introverts need time and space to think, it is better to give them topics that they can know about before, so they can answer questions and respond thoughtfully.

8. Don't Feel the Need to "Fix" Them

If introverts are to succeed in a company, they need to be addressed humanely and sincerely by their colleagues and supervisors. Not everyone should think that a person needs to be bubbly, friendly, and outgoing. Introverts have unique personalities that should be respected. Therefore, it is crucial that we don't feel the need to "fix" them to make companies more profitable. Instead, we should allow introverts to do what they do best, thinking, reflecting, and getting the job done. Introverts have an important contribution to today's companies. We should give them a chance. They can do an excellent job and can do their best for their career.

CASE STUDY #1: JASON

Jason is an introvert, and he doesn't easily get along with people. He can be shy when you first meet him. He often doesn't initiate conversations with others out of fear of being judged or misunderstood. Like many socially awkward introverts, Jason needed time and space to grow and develop. He wasn't a natural go-getter. He needed some assistance and help to engage with the people around him.

What made things difficult for Jason was the fact that he had low self-esteem and confidence, which he needed to build. With further training, he would gain a sense of self-confidence that he didn't have before. Jason took a public speaking course through an online academy. He met online with his classmates and tutor, who guided him through the entire process of learning about public speaking. Jason was terrified of making a mistake in front of others, and he would often berate himself after giving a speech. As he started to write his speeches, he began to feel more confident. He got some good feedback from his classmates and tutor, which helped him improve gradually over time. Jason was also scared of watching himself on a camera, but he started to film himself and immediately noticed what he was doing on screen. It helped him become more self-aware, especially of the tics that he knew were making him feel awkward. Later, he was able to remove those from his overall appearance, and it made a big difference.

After a whole semester of public speaking training with the online course, Jason was ready to start making speeches at work in front of his coworkers. When the company had something for him to present, he was more inclined to do it and less worried about making mistakes in front of others. His supervisors and colleagues gave him enough time to prepare his presentations, so he could easily get everything together, including his PowerPoints and other media. Soon, Jason's self-confidence skyrocketed. He was no longer afraid of making presentations and giving speeches. Instead, he exuded an air of experience and enthusiasm. He was able to surmount his fear of public speaking and demonstrate competence in his field. Overall, it could be said that Jason had become a successful introvert by utilizing a skill that he didn't know he had and developing his talents so he could meaningfully contribute to his company. It was a success story.

CASE STUDY #2: EMILIE

Emilie was a highly skilled and knowledgeable professional with a set of impeccable attributes, including being hard-working, cheerful, and willing to go above and beyond for everyone involved. The one thing she lacked: small talk and social skills. It was one of the things that made Emilie go home and bawl her eyes out after work. She was unhappy that she could not engage with others around her.

One aspect of her life that she dreaded was going to conferences for her work, where she would immediately have to meet hundreds of new people that she had never seen before. Networking was not her strength, and she wanted to bury herself in a book or go outside and take a solitary walk between sessions of the conference. Emilie wanted to improve in the area of small talk, but she didn't know where to start. She felt that something was holding her back from getting where she wanted to be.

One of Emilie's good friends was Pam. Pam was a socialite who went out all the time with her friends and wanted to have a good time. Pam knew how to do small talk and she had a lot of experience with networking at her job. She was able to give Emilie some tips on how to engage with people in small talk.

Here's what she told Emilie. "Emilie, I think that you just need to relax and be yourself. You're a talented woman with a lot of accolades to your name. Be confident. Share your achievements with others. Engage others with your charm and intelligence. I'm sure there will be people who want to meet you and befriend you. When you're at conferences, connect with people on their level. When you find something in common with someone, then you can immediately have a conversation, not too deep, but just enough for you to bond. It's not easy to make connections with others, but once you do, you will find that it's not that hard to start a conversation with someone. All you need is a little bit of advanced preparation and some go-to topics and then you're all set. You can talk to others and you might make a friend or two."

After talking with Pam, Emilie felt a lot better and wanted to take her up on her advice. Emilie approached conferences with more confidence. By preparing some topics, including doing some advanced research on the conferences she would be attending, Emilie found it a lot easier to talk to people. Having read up on the different seminars, she was able to talk to her networking contacts with ease. Indeed, she found that it was easy to flip out her card and give it to the people who were at the conference. Pretty soon, Emilie collected a whole stack of business cards from the different conferences she attended, which enabled her to expand her circle and have more people with whom she could be in contact. With her skills and experience and self-esteem boost, Emilie was ready to go to the next level in her career.

TAKING BACK OWNERSHIP OF YOUR CAREER

As you can see in the cases of Jason and Emilie, developing people skills is crucial to getting you where you need to be. Although Jason and Emilie were not natural "people persons," they were able to develop important social skills through the mentorship and training of other people, who were more knowledgeable in this area. They took ownership of their career and were able to overcome the challenges that were in the way.

We should not let our personalities, weaknesses, or other matters get in the way of where we want to go. Sure, life is tough and we may find it difficult to achieve our goals. But one of the most important aspects of improving ourselves is through our relationships with other people. Developing people skills will help us move from one echelon of understanding to a new level of career.

If you're not moving forward in your career, you're moving backward. Don't allow yourself to stagnate. Improve yourself. Don't settle for less. You can achieve your goals, but you have to take ownership of your career. You have to want to get better. It's vital to find ways to challenge ourselves. Hard work and dedication are key to succeeding in this competitive world. Therefore, by developing your people skills, you're more likely to succeed in climbing the corporate ladder and building meaningful relationships. Your earning potential can increase substantially, and you may very well find yourself in a career that you love and want to stay in for a long time.

Confidence and "Fake It Until You Make It"

Have you ever wondered how to build confidence and become a "people person?" Then, think about the old adage, "Fake it until you make it." Often, we aren't confident, so we must act like we are in order to appear competent. It is not easy, but once you allow yourself to falter and make some mistakes, you will find that you will continuously gain confidence. At first, it is difficult, and even scary because and you will find yourself suffering from "imposter syndrome." But it can be a very useful tactic to get you through initial stages of something new.

You embody people skills by becoming genuinely interested in other people. There are too many self-absorbed people in this world, who only care about their own affairs and want to simply masquerade around and share their ideas at the expense of others. But you don't have to be that way. Show humility and ask questions to people to show that you are intrigued by them, and then offer them something special: your expertise. By connecting with others, you will find that you can easily engage in conversations that will show your competence and make you much more credible and worth listening to, which increases your self-confidence and the impression you make on others.

Not everyone is a natural "people person." However, you can do it by getting out of your comfort zone, even if it is only for an hour or two. Allow your guard down and let yourself feel the excitement of trying something new. Sometimes, all it takes is simply taking a risk and going for it. What do you have to lose? If you want to advance your career, you have to be invested in people to facilitate your growth and development.

KEY TAKEAWAYS

To sum up, it is vital to develop your people skills. It doesn't come naturally to everyone, but it is a necessary part of building your career. Don't just sit there; do something to improve your people skills. Go out and meet people. Take a risk. Fake it till you make it. You will feel better about yourself the more you put yourself out there. It's not going to be easy at first. You may feel self-conscious and unable to take the first step. But once you leave your comfort zone and enter into the corporate world, you will find that you can make your way and find your calling and a place to be. It will soon become your element. You will be talking naturally to your colleagues, networking contacts, supervisors, literally everyone you meet, because you know how to connect with them on a human and professional level. The way of the future is engaging with others, and it is going to lead you to become a much more socially adept professional who will succeed in his or her career and life, in general. You can take all these skills and use them for the rest of your life. Do it for you; do it for your career! You won't regret it one bit. You can do it!

5

HOW TO MANAGE YOUR CURRENT JOB WHILE LOOKING FOR ANOTHER

Perhaps, now you have realized that you have not been "owning your career" and you are going to need to do what you can to fulfill your purpose in this life. This chapter will focus on providing you with the tools and techniques you need to handle any chaos along the way as you pursue your goals and dreams. Further, it discusses the fact that not everyone at your job needs to know that you've recently had this profound realization, and it asserts that bridges are better left unburnt until they are fully crossed. This chapter will acknowledge the potential hardships within this transition period and further highlight that this is commonly where most people "give up"... but it will also show you that you can push through and make it work.

Let's look at different ways you can smooth the process of looking for a new job while you're still at your current employer.

DO NOT LET ALL OF YOUR CO-WORKERS KNOW YOU'RE APPLYING FOR A NEW JOB

When it comes to looking for new positions, timing is everything, and it can become difficult when you want to talk about your impending departure and what it will look like for your workplace. You have to watch your every move and ensure no one else will notice that you are looking at new workplaces. It can be useful to reflect on how you typically act within the workplace in order to ensure that you can avoid doing anything differently during the transition period. You need to be as careful as possible and not "out" yourself at a moment's notice.

When you feel that you want to move on to a new job, you might feel the need to tell others about your departure. Do not! You know that saying from World War II that says, *"loose lips sink ships?"* If you open up too soon then you might jeopardize your chances of keeping your current job or lose out on future opportunities, as well. An exception to this rule is if there are layoffs at your company and your current boss wants to help you in the process of finding a new job.

It is best to keep your personal revelations to yourself whenever you understand what your goals in your life are and what you can do to achieve them. Maintain your privacy and do your job, but don't let people into your space who don't need to be there. It will only add fuel to the furnace and make you more susceptible to ending with bad relationships with others and potentially burnt bridges.

APPLY OUTSIDE OF NORMAL WORK HOURS

It takes a long time to search for a new job, and it is a full-time job. But you should resist all temptation to look for a new position while you're at your company laptop. You could be accused of time theft if you're clocking in and looking for new companies to work for or researching your new business idea. It is almost certain that looking for a new job at your current workplace is not going to be successful anyway because the job search requires you to be focused on the task at hand. You cannot get distracted. If you're worried about being found out, you're wasting your time because you're not giving the task of job searching the time and energy required. Instead, you're distracted by getting your current work done while trying to look for a new job. It is meaningless and pointless (Smith, 2013).

USE YOUR PERSONAL EMAIL ACCOUNT AND CELL PHONE

To keep yourself anonymous and undercover, it is vital for you to limit all communication about your job search to your own devices, including your personal email account and cell phone. Do NOT use a company's phone or email account to make your inquiries about job opportunities. It will send red flags to your boss and potentially get you sacked. Try to do all of your job searching offsite at your home or in a cafe, where no one could possibly find out you're doing it. Try to keep it separate from your work life. If you need to answer a job search-related phone call, take an extended lunch break and tell your boss that you need some personal time before going back to work (Murphy, 2017).

TAKE A PERSONAL DAY FOR YOUR INTERVIEW

Next, it is important for you to take a personal day for your interview. Don't lie to your employer and tell them you're sick and can't come to work, which could send mixed signals and make it questionable for you. Above all, your ethical conduct is important, and you don't want to send the wrong message by taking a sick day, which could be used legitimately if you were to fall ill for any reason. Instead, take a personal day out of your schedule. You can use it for any reason, and your employer will not question you on it because everyone needs a day off from time to time. But don't send any signals that you're applying for a job or doing an interview during that time. Maintain a low profile and don't publicize any of your actions on Facebook or any kind of media online (Murphy, 2017).

DO NOT CHANGE THE WORKLOAD YOU TAKE ON

Once a person decides he or she wants to leave the workplace for a new job, they might think that they can just coast through another month or even year and not do anything more than get by and do the bare minimum. Some people will naturally work less at this point, while others will overcompensate. It is important for you to realize that you need to maintain a steady course and maintain your work responsibilities, to the best of your ability. Don't allow yourself to slide into mediocrity for several months; it will only come back to bite you. Simply put, you need to do everything to see yourself improving in your current job; any kind of backsliding will hurt your career trajectory in the long run.

Maintaining secrecy and privacy during a job search is

challenging., but it is vital for you not to mention the fact that you're leaving to others in the office or in other public forums or social media accounts. It would be wise to work with people in your networks with whom you trust for their discretion and who can help you in your search.

CASE STUDY: ADELE

Adele was an adept, tech-savvy administrative assistant, who had worked hard at her current position but was actively looking for jobs on her own time. She continued working as hard as she could and tried to earn new accolades and score a raise or two, even while she thinking about all the other things she wanted to do with her life. Eventually her patience and perseverance paid off. She was able to share her news with her existing colleagues she had finally landed a job as a flight attendant, which she had always wanted to do.

Want to know the secret of how Adele did it? What made Adele successful was how she was able to get flight-attendant training and interviews done on the weekends. She kept her distance from her coworkers and did not tell them about the possibility of leaving until she had accepted an official offer from a new employer.

YOUR BOSS SHOULD BE THE FIRST TO KNOW ABOUT YOUR NEW POSITION

Once you've landed a new position, the first person who should know about your departure is your boss. This shows that you have respect and demonstrates your willingness to collaborate on the exit strategy. You should approach your boss from a place of positivity, love, and understanding. Show them how much you have appreciated their leadership, even if it hasn't been the best. Do not bad mouth or complain about any situation. Instead, stay positive as you tell them about your timeline for leaving. You are not obligated to anyone at your current company to reveal your next move, unless of course, you are in the position of breaking an employment contract that may require signing non-compete or other legal documents, depending on your situation.

CASE STUDY: MELINDA

When Melinda knew that she was going to go back to graduate school to get her Ph.D., she was very excited about her prospects and getting out of her current dead-end job, but she did not want to advertise it to the people around her. Instead, she wanted to keep it a secret for as long as possible, and when she was accepted to her first-choice school, she held off from sharing on social media about it or even notifying her coworkers. Instead, she first gave notice at work that she would be leaving in two months to move to Boston to attend Harvard. It was a careful move that was wise, and Melinda knew that she needed to do everything she could to avoid burning bridges. Once her boss knew, she felt free to tell others around her to inform them about her departure, which made it better for everyone. In the end, Melinda made a great decision.

ENVISION THE TRANSITION PERIOD

As you're waiting for your departure, it is crucial for you to maintain your course and energy, even though you might feel like you're in a slump and made the wrong decision. Once you've decided to hit the door next week, month, or year, it is not the time to stagnate or give in to the temptation to simply coast your way to the finish line. Instead, you need to practice "tuning in" and pay attention to all the tasks that require your care. You need to stay on your hunches and continue to work at your present company. Life has not ended and you are not going to be leaving anytime soon.

You need to be working all the way to the last minute you are at your current employer. Be patient, because that day will come soon enough. You should take care of all your job responsibilities and perform them to the very best of your ability because you want to make the strongest possible last impression to others in your company. As mentioned above, it is best to not burn any bridges.

Think About Training a Replacement

When you're thinking about your way out of a work situation, you might only be thinking about yourself and what you can do about your situation. But if you have an inkling of respect and concern for your fellow coworkers and the establishment you have been a part of, then you should make every effort to train your replacement. This will show that you are intent on helping your company in the transition process, which could be a bit rocky and require time, money, and investment of various human resources. If you have someone in mind that you could recommend taking your position, it would be a wise decision to talk to your supervisor. Try to be as helpful as possible during the transition period. Take on extra responsibilities. Prepare tutorials and other resources that will help your successor take on your job capacities. This will show that you are mature and caring. While you might only be thinking about your own work affairs, it shows a lot of character and integrity if you show interest in helping others by making your transition as seamless as possible.

When you are on your way out the door, offer support and training to your successor. Spend a day or two talking to him or her about what you have done in the office and what they can expect from day one at the office. Try to be a mentor and give the most salient advice to him or her, which will encourage future job success and show investment in the company. Walk your successor step by step through your schedule and your everyday responsibilities, so they can see what a day in your life looks like and can imagine taking on your role. Offer to be on-call for the first week or two while your successor is getting settled so you can answer any questions he or she might have.

Most people would not go the extra mile to help their replacement integrate into their role, but if you really care about the people in your company, then it would be wise for you to do everything you can to make your successor comfortable when starting to work in your position. For lower functions, training is simply not a priority for most companies, but you can stand out and offer the support that could be exactly what someone needs to fill your shoes and provide stability in a company. It makes a huge difference. Think of it as a way of mentoring and providing support, as well as empathy and altruism. These attributes are essential to have a lasting career impact in the world.

Leave on the Best Possible Terms

It is important for you to leave a place better than you found it, and you also need to be mindful that you are leaving a space that someone else will fill for you. By making everything good for your successor, you can do your best to ensure that the transition process is completely successful. It is vital for you to find a way to have a graceful and positive exit strategy because that will make life easier for you and for everyone around you.

Finally, after you've successfully left your workplace, you might have a time gap of a few months or weeks. You should do all you can to stay on course during that time and complete the things you need to so you won't fall flat and become complacent. Try to keep yourself busy and do tasks that will require a lot of energy, which will enable the time to pass by faster.

KEY TAKEAWAYS

It is evident that preparing for your next career move will require dedication, strategy, and patience. When you're getting ready to turn in your notice, you have to watch your every move and consider how your actions, both nonverbal and verbal, will come across to everyone with whom you work. You have to be mindful of how you're being perceived at work and the things you can do to be the most efficient and inspiring worker at your workplace. Don't take for granted the fact that you are in a privileged position in that you are looking for work while currently employed. Make sure that your boss is the first to know about your new position and think about making your departure easier on the company by training your replacement. By following these steps, you give yourself the best chance of staying on good terms with your former coworkers.

6

CLIMBING THE CORPORATE LADDER

S o, you want to move up the corporate ladder, do you? Many Americans dream of making it to the top. It is the American Dream, after all, to have the best job with the greatest amount of job security, as well as a paycheck that ensures your retirement will be the best it can be and you won't have to work another day in your life when you're done. While most people want to make it up the corporate ladder, it is very hard to do so and can take a long time to accomplish. Before we go into how you can climb the corporate ladder, let's talk about the organizational structure of it.

THE ORGANIZATION OF THE CORPORATE LADDER

Within a corporation or company, there is a hierarchy of different positions that go from the bottom up. At the bottom of the ladder are the entry-level positions, which are the jobs of people just starting their careers. This layer is also called the employee level, which is where the majority of workers are. In this layer, there is typically a lot of turnover, and the job is shuffled periodically. Usually, entry-level jobs evolve into more senior management roles over time, but it can take several years.

After 2-5 years of employment as an employee, it is possible to move up to the management layer of the corporate ladder. Here, you have your assistant manager, associate manager, and senior management roles, which all have varying degrees of responsibilities and must report to the higher-ups. Most people end up in these roles but struggle to move up farther because there are far fewer roles at the top.

At the top, there are the executive functions of a company, which include the executive assistant, vice-president, and president of a corporation. These roles are few and far between; however, they are the most coveted. Many Americans long to be in this position, but few ever achieve it. But with hard work and perseverance, a person could reach this level after 10+ years in a management position.

As you can see, the corporate ladder is a large hierarchy, and it includes many steps. Many people remain in the same layer for a long period of time but cannot move to other points. Instead, they get stuck somewhere and have to simply settle and keep doing their work at that level (The Corporate Ladder: Definition, Structure, and Positions, n.d.).

What Does the Corporate Ladder Actually Look Like?

The corporate ladder varies by industry and field, and different companies operate in several different ways. The typical position will evolve over time; however, it will only advance one step at a time. Rarely would there be a position that shifts from a lower position to an extremely high position. Instead, it changes gradually, so people have to remain in a position for a long time to see any kind of results.

HOW TO DEAL WITH BEING UNDERVALUED

Perhaps, you're thinking that you are not valued at work. You think of your lowly position and imagine the possibilities, but you have no luck in finding something you're passionate about. Instead of moping around and complaining, you should find ways to get people to like you. Do that by showing interest in other people and asking them how they're doing. Give people compliments and encouragement and always smile at work. Don't be a Negative Nancy and instead promote a spirit of optimism and positivity. This kind of attitude goes a long way and will help you cope with feelings of resentment toward the people in higher positions.

Instead of focusing on where you want to be in a company, think about how you can be the best person for your position. How can you improve your skill sets, get the education you need, or mentor another employee who is in your position? Think of all the ways you can improve your resume and add sections that will help you snag a better position at a higher layer of the corporate ladder. We always need to be looking for ways we can improve ourselves, and the more you focus on that, you will feel more valued and you can appreciate your own strengths and weaknesses in the process.

SELF-REFLECTION

Now, it's self-reflection time. Think about how you are

doing in your current position. Ask yourself a few questions and do a self-inventory.

1. Have you actually been doing as good as you convince yourself?

In this question, you have to consider your current skill set and how you're conducting yourself at work. What are you doing to improve your functions? Are you doing well? How was your last performance evaluation? Did you get some good feedback from that? Consider the areas where you have weaknesses and where you can improve, but also think about the areas you are particularly strong at, including time management and detail orientation.

2. Could you be more expansive and forward-thinking?

Think about your goals and aspirations. How do you see your current role evolving, improving, or expanding? Where do you see yourself in one year, two years, or more? You need to think about everything step by step and about where you want to go in your career. Paris or New York were not built in a day. Your career will likewise take a lot of time, but you can be the architect of your future. Let your creative juices and energy flow forth, and you will see the possibilities of your future.

Assess the Status of Your Coworkers

Think about your coworkers and what they are doing. Are they also looking to expand their unique skill sets or traits? Do they want to move forward like you? Are you surrounded by like-minded individuals, or do you have a lot of apathetic colleagues who could care less about improving themselves?

You should also think about how you can do things better than your colleagues. What are some ways you can improve that can outdo the level of work your coworkers are doing? Consider the ways you can outperform your unmotivated peers. It might just make them work harder and have more ambition. Ultimately, however, your internal motivation is going to be the biggest thing that keeps you going. But once it's started, it's going to be contagious, and others will want to catch on, as well. Make a difference in your workplace. You might be the light that shines in the darkness to bring forth a new wave of ambitious workers.

What Is the Source of Your Validation?

At the end of the day, if we live by the praise of humans, we will die for the praise of humans. We all want to be affirmed, loved, and applauded by others. It's human nature, and we want to be liked. That's normal. But not everyone is going to be liked or applauded by others. In fact, many of us are going to be left idle or rejected by the world. Performance evaluations and other markers of our achievement may be the things you live for, but they are not going to make you successful. Instead, it is your own pursuit of development and happiness that is going to get you there. That comes from deep within you. The best workers are conscientious, goal-driven, and centered people who believe in themselves and know they can achieve their dreams if they try hard enough. If you're living for someone else's expectations of you, then you're probably not living the life you're meant to be living. Instead, you should find ways to love yourself, push yourself, and believe that you're worth it. You can only be truly and 100% accepted by you, so look at yourself in the mirror and enjoy seeing the wonderful creation you were meant to be in this world. Having this joy and peace will be the way that you can live a truly fulfilled life.

THINK ABOUT HAVING A BLUEPRINT AND PLAN FOR WHERE YOU WANT TO GO

Continue to do some self-reflecting and think about what you want to do in your next steps. Why do you want to pursue this job? What do you hope to reap from it? Here, you have to consider your motivations and goals and see if they align with the job you are applying for. A lot of people go through their lives not knowing what they want. Maybe they want job security, a nice large paycheck, or comfortable benefits. They only think about the means to an end, but they don't consider the end itself. You have to think about what it is you ultimately are living your life for. Is it for this job or something else? Ask yourself the hard questions. It's important for you to be intuitive and self-reflective, especially as you think about what you want to do with your life.

Next, you should think about having a blueprint and plan in place of how you intend to reach where you want to go. Plan it out step by step, year by year, if you need to, and try to be as detailed as possible. Think back to the old adage, "Having no plan is a plan to fail." If you have no plan, chances are, you aren't going to see the results you want. But when you have that blueprint that you have put into writing, that you can tangibly see, then you will know where you want to be. It won't be a big "?" on your paper. Instead, you will see the visible lines of your goals and steps to reach them, which will help you realize your dreams. Commit to everything and do it all to the best of your ability. And you will see the results you deserve to receive.

"With more power comes more responsibility." Are you willing to have more responsibility? Many daydream of climbing the corporate ladder. Many think that all their dreams will come true once they become a business executive or president of a company. But what people don't tell you is just how much stress and anxiety comes at that level. While you may be happy to get the pay raise, are you willing to go to a higher step on the ladder just because of the monetary component? Think carefully about where you tread and how far you go up. It is hard to juggle all the responsibilities and unique stressors that come with having a higher position on the scale. A lot of things tip on your shoulders. Knowing how to manage people becomes difficult and extremely challenging. Having less time off might also not be very easy. Many people just cannot handle the extra stress of a ton of functions they have to do. Do you want that level of responsibility? It's important to know exactly what you want in a job and not just a paycheck or a benefits package. You have to know that a job is the right one for you.

TOOLS AND TECHNIQUES FOR STANDING OUT IN YOUR CURRENT POSITION

Now, you might be wondering, "What are some ways I can stand out to beat the crowd and do my best in different situations?" Here are some tips you can follow.

1. Be a Learner

When you are positioning yourself in a company, you should always think with a growth mindset and not a static mindset. Many people get into the position where they are thinking about the future but they aren't learners. Show that you want to grow and develop. Learn how to learn, because that will help you become a better leader. True leaders are lifelong learners, and they commit to educating themselves about the latest trends and other facts about life.

Read up on and research all the latest trends in your field. Continually read, read, and read. The more you know, the more power you will have in the future. You have to have a lot of background knowledge, which will position yourself to succeed in your current working environment. Don't ever see limitations in your given current title. Instead, imagine the possibilities and your ability to grow within your role. When you learn more, your work will be able to affect change in the world around you. You will also become more prepared to move on to a higher-level role because you have continually developed your knowledge and skills (Sciortino, 2019).

2. Allow Your Work to Speak for Itself

In your current role, you should not sell your own career and self. Instead, you should focus on your growth in your role, character, and attitude, because they say everything about you. Do you go beyond what is expected of you? Do you try to do all you can to help someone in need? Do you sometimes stay extra time outside of work because you want to get the job done well? Your work ethic says a lot about you, and this kind of commitment will help you to become noticed and more likely to be promoted. The people who are most likely to succeed are those who are standout candidates, who try to do everything excellently and to their best ability. The desire to be excellent in their field extends to not just professional activities but also everyday life, as well (Sciortino, 2019).

3. Be a Team Player

As you're working on a team, you should be the best team player you can be. That means working with others and collaborating on projects with them. You cannot be on your own in a company doing things by yourself without the help of others. While certain roles lend themselves to independence and are helpful for working alone, in most corporate settings, you will have to work with other people. Having good people skills plays into it, as clear communication is crucial for both your team's success and your company's. It is crucial to communicate well with your co-workers, boss, and your team. When you do this well, then everyone can do their best in their work and the whole company benefits and prospers.

Contribute to your team and work hard. Be a reliable person that your teammates can count on. You don't want to be the person that everybody is waiting on to submit the latest assignment that is due tomorrow. Instead, you want to be proactive, diligent, and dependable. Be the best worker you can be and work for the good of others. Communicate with them in an honest and straightforward manner so that everyone will be on the same page. Show a vested interest in the community and make your presence known, even if you are a bit understated. By doing so, you can make a very effective contribution to your team and accomplish all your goals and objectives.

4. Do Every Task Gladly and Be Humble

Some people think that just because they're at a higher level on the echelon of the corporate ladder that they can do anything they want. As you move higher, you should never start telling yourself, "That's not in my job description." If you say that, it will feed into your pride and self-importance, which will not help you advance your career. Instead, you should employ a can-do attitude that wants to help others in need. See a colleague overloaded or struggling to complete a task? Kindly help him or her and pick up the slack.

You will need to stay humble as you progress up the corporate ladder. Think about the team mindset and contributing to the people in your team. Don't neglect the small things. In a company, you want everyone to succeed. Consider the welfare and status of the people around you. No longer position yourself as a solo employee in a company, but rather as a collaborator in a company, who seeks to do his or her best for others. By lifting up the people you work with, you will help the company, and thus yourself, prosper.

5. Connect With People

It is important for you to develop your investment in other people because that will set you up for success in your life. If you're able to connect with others, company leaders will notice and they will see in you a possibility to further the goals of the organization. Collaboration is important. By exercising the people skills you have developed, you will exhibit key leadership qualities that will be noticed by your employers and potentially rewarded with promotions and other rewards for which you are considered. Consider the possibilities of growth within your current workplace and environment. You might find it uncessary to move around to get where you want to be (Sciortino, 2019).

HOW TO LEVERAGE SPECIFIC OPPORTUNITIES

Here's some information on how you can leverage specific opportunities within a company.

1. Know Your Supervisor or Boss

Make yourself as likable and interesting as possible and especially get to know your supervisor. Continually tell them about what you're doing and how it's going. Management will likely notice the job you're doing, so make yourself visible to them. But you should also get to know them personally. Maintain integrity at all times and show that you respect them, as well. Also, make sure to set up regular meetings with your boss, which will help you find out about any opportunities as they arise (Rasmussen, 2016).

2. Continually Update Your Boss About Your Accomplishments

You don't have to be boastful when you talk about your accomplishments. Instead, you can communicate them with your boss in a low-key way that does not call too much attention to yourself. For example, you could send a memo with a comment from a customer that talks about their satisfaction with your service. You could say, "My client recently gave very positive feedback to me after receiving our services. She said, 'This is the best company I've ever contacted. I appreciated the human connection and value of this service and will continually go back to them and no one else.'" When you share this kind of comment with your boss, you're giving yourself external validation, which says a lot about you. And then, your boss will love you for doing that and for making the company score a client who will become a loyal customer (Rasmussen, 2016).

3. Create Your Job

If you are able to identify a gap in the business where there is a need, you can present a new idea to your boss that will benefit the company and possibly open a new opportunity for you. Make sure to present your case as a profit center or value-add. If you develop a detailed plan with estimated outcomes, you will likely be able to convince your boss to give you a new position with higher responsibilities. Who knows? You might even be in the process of creating your own dream job.

4. Step Up to New Responsibility

If you are truly ambitious, don't be shy about taking on new responsibilities. Instead, step up to the plate! If you see a project or a special task that would benefit from your expertise, go for it. The more initiative you have, the more respect you will gain from your leaders. If you can demonstrate that you can tackle responsibilities, you will be given the opportunity to take on new responsibilities and functions you didn't have before.

5. *Keep your resume and online professional profiles current at all times*

When you see a job open within your company that you want to apply for, make sure you're ready for it. Be sure you're capturing your accomplishments, including volunteer work you participate in outside of your job. Do not go back more than 10 years. Even better, apply with your resume, application, and a recorded video resume. It is becoming more and more popular for standing out after you've made it through the Artificial Intelligence screening.

KEY TAKEAWAYS

Moving up the career ladder can be important to your long-term goals but is a time-consuming process. If that is your desire, it is crucial to stay aware of the ways to advance your career. Having a vision in place and an action plan will enable you to find your next promotion within your company. Reinvent your personal brand

and remain authentic. Take advantage of opportunities to take on additional job responsibilities and stay aware of opportunities that open up either within your company or within another. Display that you are a team player by being cooperative and communicative, and above all, stay humble as you climb the corporate ladder.

7

THE INTERVIEW

This final chapter will highlight the things you can do to nail your next job interview and snag the dream job you've been waiting for. Are you ready for it? Let's get ready - the show is about to begin.

WHAT DOES AN INTERVIEW LOOK LIKE TODAY?

The Difference Between Interviews Nowadays and Those of Years Past

Interviews have changed these days. No longer are candidates left in the dark about job opportunities because they can find out a lot more about the company than before, thanks to the Internet. Researching company culture is easier than ever, which means that there is no excuse for not knowing about a company.

Conversely, companies can find out more about people through a simple Google search. This can be either helpful or hurtful to the job candidate, which is why you need to be careful about your every move on the Internet and not reveal too much information that could disqualify you from a position.

Additionally, there is a lot more competition these days for positions because people can easily find out about the opportunities that are available to them around the world. Therefore, you need to look online. There are endless positions to be found. You just have to look for them, and you have to stand out because there is a sea of applicants waiting at the door.

Finally, many interviews are now being conducted using technology. Skype interviews and Zoom meetings are becoming more common. Often, the interview process begins with a Skype interview to weed out undesirable candidates and then proceeds to an in-person interview. Because of technology, companies can find the best possible candidates to interview on-site, which increases competition and makes the job application smoother and more efficient.

The Newest Most Sought-After Skills

With all the latest interview processes becoming more streamlined and efficient, employers have some new qualities they are looking for in candidates. They seek candidates who have a good personality and those that can relate to others through emotional intelligence.

Emotional intelligence is the ability to relate to others' emotions and regulate and utilize one's own emotions. Empathy has become a valuable skill in the workplace. The more you know about how to connect with people on an emotional level, the more likely you will be perceived as relatable and personable. Additionally, you can support the mission of the company by being a positive and caring person who contributes to the company culture in ways that will build others up.

Another aspect that is important is an individual's social skills. By showing yourself to be relatable and approachable, you will demonstrate competence in people skills. Such skills are important for being able to network and share ideas with your colleagues, which many companies look for in their candidates.

WHAT DOES A GOOD INTERVIEW LOOK LIKE?

All interviews begin with the job application process. You send in your resume and follow up with HR, and you get the interview and arrange it by phone or email.

Interviews can take place with one person asking you the questions or with a panel. And they can be individual or group interviews. Many interviews will last no longer than one hour, while some will last only thirty minutes. But with many interviews, the longer it lasts, the better the impression you have made.

For any job interview, first impressions are *everything*. Make a wrong move or take a bad turn and you will ruin your chances of getting past the interview. Take steps to get there and you will be in the interview of your dreams.

1. Punctuality

The first point you should consider is being on time. Show respect to your potential supervisors and HR people by arriving at the interview site early. Scout out where the interview will take place. Potentially take a tour of the site beforehand, so you can figure out what building and room your interview will take place in. This is a simple one, and you need to be on time because that will be the first point to guarantee a good interview.

2. Dress the Part

The second aspect of the first impression is your dress code. Consider what people wear in the company you're looking at and dress the part, but up a notch. If your company requires a shirt and tie for men, wear a formal suit. If your company requires ladies to wear a dress, do so and make it your Sunday best. Polish yourself and show the image you want to convey to your audience. Put some gel or hair spray in your hair, take a good, long shower in the morning, and put on some nice perfume, but don't make it too strong. Project yourself as a professional who is serious and who really wants the job.

3. Confidently Prepare With Questions and Research

A good interview includes a candidate who has done his or her research thoroughly for the interview. When you know your stuff, you will show yourself to be a standout candidate, who has not only read the job board and advertisement but has looked into the company itself and examined why it is a good fit for you. A good interview candidate demonstrates knowledge of the mission statement of the company, the company culture, as well as the product line offered. You should also prepare excellent questions you can ask at the interview to inquire more about the things that may not appear on the company website, which shows your demonstrated interest in the company.

4. Conduct Yourself Professionally

A successful candidate conducts himself or herself

professionally through the entire interview. Shake hands and thank your interviewer for taking the time to speak with you. Demonstrate poise with your shoulders back and show good posture throughout the interview. Lean into your interviewer to show proximity and relatability.

5. Be Authentic

The successful interview has a candidate who is authentic and presents himself or herself with integrity and authenticity. Nothing is worse than having a candidate who is not prepared or someone who lies to cover things up in an interview. The interviewers can see right through that, and they will not hire you if you do that. Be yourself. It's a simple concept but one that works.

6. Begins and Ends With Gratitude

Finally, a good interview begins and ends with gratitude. You thank the interviewer at the beginning and the end of the interview. And you follow-up with a thank you note after the interview is over. Showing thankfulness demonstrates humility and appreciation, which are desirable attributes in a job candidate.

WHAT DOES A BAD INTERVIEW LOOK LIKE?

On the other hand, a bad interview looks like the total opposite. Here are some attributes of a bad interview.

1. The Candidate Is Late

At a bad interview, a candidate is late for the interview. One or two minutes is forgivable, but five, ten, or twenty minutes is unacceptable. Nothing ruins a first impression more than being late for the interview.

2. You're Underdressed or Overdressed

Dress code is important for an interview. If you find yourself in a situation where you are significantly underdressed or overdressed, you will leave a bad impression and they will not give you the job. Prepare well beforehand for this aspect. There is nothing worse than arriving at an interview only to realize you wore the wrong clothes. It completely detracts from your image and makes you less confident.

3. You're Not Prepared

If you have no plan, you have a plan to fail. It's just that simple. You must be ready to do your best. If you have not looked at the company website and ask questions that can be answered there, then you're not ready for the interview, and it's going to flop. You asked for it - you got it.

4. You Lie a Lot

Liars and cheaters do not win. And if you lie on your resume or in the interview, the interviewer will find out sooner or later, and it could result in major consequences, not the least of which would be your impending termination from the company. Nobody likes a liar or a cheat, so don't try to do that to impress at your interview.

5. No Follow-up or Gratitude

A thankful candidate is always appreciated, and if you don't show that you're glad to be there and that you're thankful that you got the interview, then you're showing selfishness and entitlement, neither of which are desirable attributes in a candidate. Be grateful and show it to your interviewer.

TOOLS AND TECHNIQUES TO CARRY WITH YOU INTO AN INTERVIEW

Your first impression is the first image that you project to prospective employers, and it is often unforgivable. If you show yourself to be authentic, confident, and empathetic, you will likely be perceived as a good candidate. On the other hand, if you seem to be a nervous, self-conscious, and hesitant candidate, you won't be going to the next stage in the interview. It is important to appear competent and emotionally intelligent through the whole process because then you will score points with your interviewer and potentially get to the next step in the process.

Here are some tips you can carry with you to the interview to help you make a good impression and ace the interview, based on some tricks that were introduced by Shana Lebowitz, a Business Insider correspondent (Lebowitz, 2018).

1. Schedule Your Interview for a Tuesday in the Late Morning

Tuesdays tend to be the days when the interviewer is more relaxed and can be more focused on the interview process. A good time is 10:30 AM, which is after the morning grind and start of work.

2. Tailor Your Responses Based on the Age of the Interviewer

Different age ranges expect different things from job candidates, and you would do well to know what you should share with different ages. For example, for Generation X (between the ages of 20 and 30), you should talk about your ability to multitask and share a work sample or portfolio demonstrating your competence and skills. These days, Generation X managers expect someone who is tech-savvy, as well. For those who are between the ages of 30 and 50, they might expect someone who is a team player, demonstrates creativity and has a positive work-life balance. For those older than 50, you might do well to emphasize your loyalty and commitment to company culture and respect for the accomplishments of your interviewer.

3. Connect With Your Interviewer

Connection is important, especially in interviews. Find something in common with your interviewer. It might be that you both like sports or have watched the latest episode of a show on Netflix. Or, perhaps, you could talk about the news story that is getting all the attention. Try to be personable, and that will score you points with your interviewer.

4. Mirror the Body Language of the Interviewer

If the interviewer is leaning forward, then you should do the same. It is a psychological effect, which demonstrates interest in the other person. Generally, people like it whenever someone acts like them because they want to be respected and honored. It is also flattering to see this mimicry, although your interviewer might not be paying much attention.

5. Compliment the Interviewer and Company

It is important to show respect to your interviewer. Complimenting him or her without self-promotion is a good way to show your interest in them. Moreover, you want to talk about the positive aspects of the company that have attracted you to it and how you can imagine yourself working for the company.

6. Be Honest About Your Weaknesses

Although you might be tempted to share all your accomplishments with the interviewer, you should show some deference, as well. Be candid about your weaknesses when the interviewer asks about them. Don't shy away from telling something that is difficult for you. It shows your humanity and honesty. Everyone has a weakness; don't pretend you don't have any of them. But what you should do is talk about how this weakness is an area you feel you want to tackle and grow from, and that will project confidence and a growth mindset.

WHAT TO LOOK OUT FOR IN AN INTERVIEW

While it's important for you to know your stuff, it's also vital that you watch out for some things in an interview. For example, there may be some red flags about the company that might make you reconsider taking a job offer from the company. Case and point, the salary might be lower than reported in the job advertisement. Or, the interviewer might indicate that there is a high turnover rate, and that demonstrates that the company culture is not very inviting. In addition, you might experience some dishonesty or misrepresentation of facts that don't align with what you've found on the company website. Beware of those types of interviewers.

In addition, there might be some curveball questions that come your way. For example, the interviewer might ask you how you handled a situation where you were stressed and had a conflict at work. This type of question is tricky, because you might not be expecting it, and you don't want to answer something like, "I have never had a work conflict." Another curveball might be this question: "What is your greatest professional achievement?" You might feel the need to rattle off things on your CV, but you should mention something that is not on your CV that your interviewer could not find out just by looking at your info. Be creative and authentic. Finally, another question that might throw people off is, "Do you have any questions for me?" It might be tempting to say, "No, you've given me enough information." But the interviewer is expecting you to ask a few questions at the end, so be prepared with your questions in tow and get them out at the end of the interview.

HOW TO ACE ANY INTERVIEW

To add to the tips we have mentioned, it is important for you to be prepared to answer all questions. Master the basics and prepare for the hard questions. Consider the brain teasers that you could have thrown at you, and don't be rattled by them. Be as creative and innovative as possible. Practice at home your answers to questions, preferably in front of a mirror. You could even watch yourself on camera and see your poise and responses to questions, which will make you more self-aware on interview day.

It is vital for you to appear confident, even when you're not feeling it. "Fake it til you make it." This will show that you have a can-do attitude and are willing to grow and develop for the sake of the company. Also, if you feel stumped on a question, ask for a breather. Take a timeout and ask if your interviewer can return to the question later in the interview. It is better to take your time and answer a question thoughtfully, rather than ramble on and on and stumble over your words, which shows a lack of organization and authenticity.

Lastly, prepare carefully crafted questions that show a

demonstrated interest in the company and that reveal the depth of research and insight on your part. It will certainly impress the interviewer and make you a top candidate. And, don't forget to follow up the interview with a thank you note and request for next steps. By following these tips, you're guaranteed to ace the interview (EF, n.d.).

CASE STUDY: MARK

Mark was determined to succeed in his interview. He knew what he wanted to do and how to achieve it. He had thoroughly researched his company and knew the mission statement. He carefully wrote out his answers to potential interview questions in advance and created a list of twenty questions that he could ask at the interview. He bought a nice suit on sale at the local mall. He got a haircut beforehand and had his hair nice and polished. Mark looked like a gentleman when he walked into the interview. Smiling, he shook hands with the panel of interviewers and prepared for battle.

Concentrating on his interviewers and making a personal connection with each of them, he showed his charming personality, poised with grace and candor. With his knowledge of the company, he blew away the interviewers, who thought to themselves, "How did he know all this information? It's great!" Mark continually praised the company and told them how he felt the company would align with his personal goals and mission statement. He echoed the words from the website, which showed the depth of his research and interest. At the end, he followed up with gratitude in his kind statements and firm handshakes. He quickly sent a thank-you note after the interview and asked the interviewer to indicate any next steps. Within two days, the panel had made a decision, and Mark was given the job. He got it! He owned his career and got a winning job that would look great on his CV.

What made Mark successful was his graceful confidence. He demonstrated the marks of a humble but assertive gentleman with charisma and connection. By showing both his research skills and choleric personality, he demonstrated that he knew what he was doing and that he was a true go-getter. In the end, the interviewers enthusiastically hired him, knowing that he was the man for the job. It was a wonderful experience. Want to land a dream job? Be like Mark, and you will not be disappointed - you'll be the type of person companies love to hire and give promotions to, which is going to upgrade your career to the next level.

HOW SHOULD YOU PREPARE FOR YOUR NEW SOUGHT-AFTER ROLE?

When you're getting ready to take on a new role, your preparation will begin while at your current job, and you will want to think about your exit strategy and how you can make good of your time with your current employer. You don't need to spend days daydreaming at your work computer, thinking about when you will leave and go to another company. Instead, you need to have a mentality that will "get the job done" and finish the work you have already started at your company. You will likely be extremely busy and have a lot on your plate that you will need to finish at your current job, and thinking a lot about your future job is not going to help you concentrate and finish what you've already begun at your current job. To help you with this, here are some steps you can take to ensure a steady and smooth job transition process.

Train Yourself for Your New Role

If you're an ambitious type, you are likely seeking out a role that requires more experience, training, and skills. Therefore, you need to start preparing yourself for this kind of role by training yourself. Do tutorials online, read up on your field, do an online course in management or another field you're interested in. Do everything you can to become educated and well-trained in advance of your new career move. It will make you feel more prepared to move on, and you will feel more confident when you start a new job that may require a steep learning curve. The more you know about your future position, the more prepared you will be to take on the new, challenging work responsibilities that you are likely to have and the less you will be shocked by the pace of the job.

Consider the Timeline for Your Future Job

Next, you should think about the timeline for application to your future job. Do you want to begin next month or next year? Consider your financial resources and if you will need free time or money in the coming days. Prepare yourself for the move, and take some time off, if you need to, as you get ready for your next career move. Timing is everything, and the more you know about where you're headed next, the better off you will be in your new position (Murphy, 2017).

KEY TAKEAWAYS

Good interview skills are crucial to getting the job you want. We have highlighted some basics to get you started thinking about it, but you should continue to think of ways to improve and prepare well to ace the interview. Consider practicing at mock interviews either offered by a professional organization or with those in your network. Always be prepared and authentic, remember that lying can derail even the best of interviews. Finally, capitalize on the time you have between positions to prepare for your new role. We wish you the best of luck. Do your best - it's all anyone can ask of you.

UNSTUCK YOURSELF

INTRODUCTION

"Sometimes, the one thing you need for growth
is the one thing you are afraid to do."

— SHANNON L. ADLER (TELL TRUTH
QUOTES, N.D.)

What is one thing you're afraid of? What's something
that scares the crap out of you? There are a lot of things
that scare us. The fear of the unknown is one thing that
keeps people stuck and unwilling to pursue a new
career path. The old ideal of sticking to one company
and retiring 40 or more years later is changing rapidly,
however. Today, people will go through an average of

12 job changes in their lifetime. Some of the most common reasons for seeking a new job include the potential for higher pay, better benefits, relocation to a new area, career advancement, going for a less stressful job, or leaving a team or supervisor who was toxic.

According to various U.S. surveys, people who change jobs frequently experience large increases in income (Alini, 2018). The latest data from the Workforce Vitality Report by ADP said that job switchers encountered a 4.9% pay rise every year versus a 4.3% increase for job holders (Alini, 2018). You might not think that is a lot; however, over the course of a lifetime, the numbers add up rapidly. A Forbes article talked about how if you stay in a job for more than 10 years, you can lower your overall potential earnings by about 50% (Keng, 2014). When a person changes jobs, their salary is increased by an average of 10% to 20%.

Millennials, in particular, are looking to leave their current jobs for new ones. According to a recent Gallup poll, 21% of millennials report that they have changed jobs in the past year (Adkins, n.d.). The millennial generation is looking to expand their resources and gain more earnings. But more than that, they are seeking to have meaning and engagement in their work, which often doesn't happen. In fact, only 29% of millennials report feeling engaged at work, and only

30% feel connected at their job (Adkins, n.d.). These figures point to an overwhelming number of people feeling disengaged at work, which can be damaging to any company.

Don't get me wrong, making a job change is scary. It might feel easier and more comfortable to coast and try to make things better at your current job. But those who dive in and get a new job often become happier people just because they faced their fear and went for it. You might also be considering a career change because you don't feel fulfilled in your current job. However, before you jump ship and go to a job that is just as unsatisfying, you should take an inventory of what makes you happy. Consider your core values, beliefs, hobbies and passions and let them be your guide.

What should be encouraging is new research published by GoBankingRates. One study discovered that 23% of Americans who changed their jobs regretted doing so (Power, n.d.). That means a whopping 77% did not regret it at all, because they knew they had made the right decision! So, it is likely that you will not want to go back to your old job after you've leapt to a new one.

Feeling stuck in a dead-end job can be one of the most demotivating things in the world. Regardless of age, experience or aspiration, the absence of career progress will stand in the way of feeling fulfilled, getting the financial compensation you deserve, and seeing recognition for your accomplishments. There are many reasons why a person may feel stuck professionally, and there are dozens of possible solutions.

In this book we will take a look at the professional choices we make, the biggest mistakes we commit and the missed opportunities that can contribute to the feeling of being stuck. Once these primary issues are examined you will become more aware of strategies for a proactive career path change.

Let's go.

1

THE SCARY CONCEPT OF CHANGE

Feeling professionally stuck? You're not alone. Many people go through phases of their life where they feel like there is nowhere to go. I am aware of this struggle in my own life. I went to school for an Accounting and Finance degree. Then, after graduation, I got a job right away. But then, I went for an MBA, because everyone who's anyone has an MBA, right? No way. I hated every moment of working in finance. It was pure hell for me. I felt like I was a fish out of water, literally: I was gasping for air, but I couldn't breathe. It is so hard to do something you hate. Why should we waste our time on the things that suck all the energy out of us? That's what I was thinking, and it's why I decided to take on the responsibility of helping myself and others who are in the same situation.

I realized that I love to train and coach people to grow specific skills. It brings me a lot of joy when I feel like I'm helping others, while growing alongside them. That's why I'm here for you, to give you the same training and coaching, to be your cheerleader.

WHY DO WE FEEL PROFESSIONALLY STUCK?

There are several reasons why we might feel professionally stuck. Here are some with my explanations:

Being Financially Dependent on a Mundane Job

Often, because we have a steady paycheck, we think that there is no reason for us to pack up and move. We might feel that there are bills to pay and things we need to afford to buy, because we have such a decent paycheck. We simply cannot afford to leave our jobs, because we fear the unknown of a new position.

Becoming too Comfortable

Secondly, we might find ourselves feeling way too comfortable in a position that doesn't challenge us intellectually or professionally. We might be coasting through our job and clocking in every morning, only to go through our day numbing out and simply plugging and chugging while not actually doing high quality work. Consequently, we may feel disengaged and unchallenged by the work we do because it isn't stimulating enough.

Being Employed in a Shrinking Field

Furthermore, we might also be in a shrinking field with no room for advancement and not enough jobs for everyone who comes into the field, which makes us extremely complacent and unwilling to budge from our position that guarantees job security and again, a position that pays the bills.

Believing Everybody Else is Better than You

It is also possible you might feel unable to measure up to the competition because it is a dog-eat-dog world out there. There are more people vying for the latest positions in this increasingly competitive world. You might feel demotivated because you think that you won't stand a chance against the next prodigy who went to Harvard or MIT and has outstanding recommendations or references from the people they worked with.

Believing the Job Market is Too Tough

You may be feeling that the current state of the job market is grim and tough. There are likely no opportunities out there to meet the demands, so you feel that you won't be able to improve your situation if you shift to another position in the field.

Staying in a Job That's Not in Line With Your Personal Values and Beliefs

Perhaps you are in a job that only pays the bills, but there are certain compromises you have to make because the job does not align with your personal values and beliefs. This can make things difficult for you and you might find that it is paralyzing to stay in this position. You have no earthly idea where to go, because things are tough, and you're just resistant to the idea of change.

No Clear Concept of What You Really Want

Maybe you don't have a clear idea of what you want in a new career and you find it difficult to know where to start. You haven't brainstormed your goals and objectives, and it is difficult to have a clear vision because you haven't clearly considered what steps you need to take to get there, which can lead to a dead-end street.

THE FEAR OF JOB CHANGE - WHERE DOES IT COME FROM?

Where does the fear of job change come from? Why are we scared to do what we want to do, which is to break free from our current circumstance? Let's look at some of the reasons we are afraid of career change:

Fear of How We Will Be Perceived

You might feel fear of how you will be perceived. In a survey, 33% of respondents said that they wouldn't even send a resume because they worry that they would be judged too harshly. Another 38% were incredibly anxious about the interview process. We worry about how we will be viewed or judged. What will they think about our professional experience and will it be enough to impress a recruiter? It is hard to overcome this kind of self-condemnation that we may experience in our lives.

The Devil You Know

As creatures of habit, we may find ourselves wanting to only deal with situations where we know the people and the outcomes of scenarios, but we are less likely to go for the things that are not familiar to us. Therefore, the fear of the unknown comes knocking at our doors.

Worries About Making the Wrong Choice

We may also think about the fact that we could make a costly mistake that could be a nightmare for our working life and wallets. There are a lot of choices out there, and you might find yourself paralyzed by the thought of changing to a new position, because you're indecisive. Taking risks is an important part of life, but you may find yourself wanting to stay on the safe side.

You're Simply Scared You're Not Going to Find a New Job at All

Furthermore, you might find yourself in a panic and unable to make a decision because you think that you won't find a new job at all. There might be no doors that will open for you, and that scares the crap out of you. Holding on to your steady job with income and benefits seems to be the best thing you can do, so you continue clocking in and doing your duty, thinking that you are doing the right thing for your career, and that you don't want to put yourself out there in a vulnerable place.

Your Work Has Become Your Identity

For many people work is a source of identity: a person will identify himself or herself as a teacher, administrator, or other working person. They continue to form that identity for as long as they work for a company and cannot escape its hold on their life. If they suddenly quit a job where they were in that position, they might lose their sense of calling and fulfilment, because they have been tied to that role for so long. It can be difficult. For example, a teacher may find their identity in their work as an instructor and guide who helps students. Once they are stripped of that title and go into the corporate world to try and go up the corporate ladder, they might find that they have lost their sense of calling as a teacher because they are no longer in that role. For many people, this is what they don't want to lose, their sense of purpose and meaning in what they have been doing for a while.

The decision to quit and pursue something else can easily contribute to a personal identity crisis in which you don't know what to do with yourself. You might be regretful and not want to move forward with your job change decision. Depending on your age, there also could be a fear of starting over and being the new kid on the block.

THE FEAR OF CHANGING JOBS

The fear of changing jobs is understandable, but you have to overcome it if you want to make a move. Sometimes we blow the eventual consequences out of proportion within our own minds and convince ourselves the consequences are too great. Reward never comes without risk, but let's think about the long-game and what could be the amazing benefits of moving on. Let's look at 10 steps you can take to face your anxieties and conquer them so you are positioned to make that leap:

HOW TO FACE YOUR FEARS: 10 STEPS

1. Ask Yourself, "What Is It That I Fear?"

Name what you're specifically afraid of and write it down in your notebook. Examine the fear within a fear. You may have surface level fear, but there is something deeper that needs to be looked at closer. Try to find out exactly what it is that you fear the most (Stanley, n.d.).

2. Think of Your Fear as Your Conscience

Your fear can be viewed as your conscience, which wants to guide you safely to your destination. Consider how you can achieve your goal while protecting yourself in the process. How can you be able to face your fear and commitment to your goal at the same time?

3. Write Down Your Vision and Dream

What is your goal? What is your hope and dream? Think of how you want to get there and how this is the thing that you want the most. How is your fear keeping you from going for that goal? (Stanley, n.d.)

4. Stay in the Present

You might think that there is some imminent danger

lurking around the corner. But nothing is going to happen. In all likelihood, you're going to be okay. Your decision to move on and change careers is not going to be as dangerous as you're imagining it to be. Don't be afraid. Don't ignore your fear but don't give into it either. Remind yourself of your vision and take small baby steps toward your destination (Stanley, n.d.)

5. Practice Mindfulness in Your Everyday Life

One of the most important things you can do is remain grounded in your current circumstances and keep in mind what you can control and what you cannot. Remain stoic about your life. Only allow the things that are inside your sphere of influence to be things that matter to you. Only think about YOU and what you want in your life. Don't worry about the things that are going on around you. Instead, remain grounded in what you believe about yourself and what you're capable of accomplishing and leave the rest to destiny or luck.

6. Don't Worry About What Others Think

You might be in a position where you're looking for work and all your other peers are in snazzy jobs with a 401K and are doing just fine. It might feel slightly embarrassing for you to knock on their door and ask them for job search advice. But you can frame it differently and say that you got laid off and that you're taking this time to find a better opportunity where you can use your skills and experience. When asking for help, don't feel ashamed. Everyone has been there and done that. Even though you may think you're the only one looking for work, you can face your fear and get over it (Nemko, 2015).

7. You Can Still Live for Pleasure

Often, we think of work as no fun and all the pleasures of this world as much more enjoyable. You might enjoy sleeping late, having that latte in a coffee shop, hanging out with friends, and other activities. But you don't have to give those up just because you're looking for work. Having work is an important part of your contribution to society, so you should do your work to the best of your ability. If you're working in a job, you will feel like you have more meaning to your life, and you're not simply coasting through life. Instead of relying on your mom and dad to give you constant financial support, you can make your own dough, have your own place, and live a fun and independent life. Isn't that what you've always wanted?

8. Don't Be Afraid of Getting a Job You Hate

You might have been unhappy at your current job, and you're fearful of potentially landing in the same position (Nemko, 2015). Instead of worrying about that risk, you can ask your potential employer some questions. For example, you could ask them, "Could you describe a day in the life of an employee at your company?" or "What do you want employees to accomplish in their first thirty days of employment?"

If you're offered a position at this company, ask to go see the workplace and meet your potential colleagues or employees. Get a gist of what life would be like at this company. Do you hear a lot of griping or complaining? That could be a red flag. Or, do you hear people enjoying each other's company, working hard and getting things done? You can do things in your power to gauge the thermometer of the company and know what it's like to work there, which can reduce your chances of landing a crappy gig with coworkers who are not friendly or cordial.

9. Don't be Anxious About Disappointing Others

It's possible you might feel that landing a job at a fabulous company is going to let down your current coworkers, who might feel jealous and disappointed that you're leaving them for a better workplace (Nemko, 2015). Your current colleagues might feel inferior to you, and feel like you're abandoning them by going to a new and better company. But you shouldn't be afraid of disappointing others, because you can show them that ambition and talent should be rewarded. Encourage your current colleagues to work hard at what they do and not be complacent. You might get them to walk away from a job that is not rewarding them and their talents, and make them more likely to pursue their goals and dreams.

10. Don't Fear Getting Out There

Many people fear the idea of "selling themselves" and end up not marketing themselves to others. Don't think that you have to sell yourself to other people and that it is something that is pushy or self-promoting. You don't have to do that. Realize that you have to use your resume and experience to help you land that job. You need to do some selling of your gifts and talents. Don't feel afraid to put yourself out there. You should reveal your strengths and weaknesses to your prospective employer. Don't try to hide anything. Put yourself out there and you'll be more likely to be successful in your job search (Nemko, 2015).

SUMMARY

It is vital for you to put yourself out there and not be afraid of the risks that you have to take to accomplish your dreams. There are many things that scare us and make us afraid of making our next move. But often, those fears are irrational. We need to give ourselves the space and time to go do the things that excite and motivate us. It's not easy to be motivated, but once we become vulnerable and take on our fears like we're in a boxing match, then we can punch them right in the face and give them the crushing blow, because we can do all the things we set our minds to.

You too can overcome your fears and anxieties. Don't give up. Take it one day at a time. The start is the most difficult place to be. But once you've begun something, it can lead to bigger and better things.

2

WHEN SHOULD I SEEK A CAREER CHANGE?

It's important to differentiate between issues that can be resolved and career problems that will always be there. This chapter is going to help you pinpoint the symptoms of a job that doesn't really have the potential to turn into a fulfilling career. It will outline the most important questions you will need to ask yourself to determine if you're stuck and if the time is right to pursue professional change. Let's look at some surefire signs that you need to walk out of your current job as soon as possible.

YOU DREAD GOING TO WORK

Feeling the Monday blues? Dreading getting up the next morning after your lovely and leisurely Sunday when you stayed on the couch and did nothing? You might think that every day is a struggle and you wish that your morning commute would never end. When you're at work, you keep glancing at the clock and hoping for the hours to go by faster. Let me tell you something, many people are in your shoes. They are also struggling with anxiety and lack of motivation to go to work. Too many people hate their jobs these days, and when you dread going to work, there is nothing worse than getting on that subway or bus, or fighting traffic on the highway to get to work. Been there and done that. It's a real struggle, but it is also a warning sign that something is not quite right, and you need to do some re-evaluation to see if working in this job is worth it in the end.

YOU FEEL LIKE A ROBOT

There's nothing worse than feeling like a cog in a gigantic machine that is your company. You might think you're plugging and chugging at work and always trying to get the job done to the best of your ability. But when there's no passion or creativity to get you going at work, then you're probably in a dead-end job which is not going to provide you with the challenge it takes to succeed and get ahead. If you find yourself on "autopilot" all the time and handling your professional responsibilities without thinking, then you've got to start thinking about your exit strategy and moving on to bigger and better things. A lack of challenge is also something that is going to make you stagnate and not get any better at what you do. When you're complacent, you're going to miss out, as your job prospects become dimmer when you don't challenge yourself to get out and do something to advance your career.

YOU FEEL TRAPPED

Next, you may feel trapped in your current position, thinking that there is no way to move forward and out of your current circumstances. Chances are you feel stuck and you need a career change right now, but you're unsure how to make your move. The feeling of emotional and psychological paralysis is enough of a warning sign to tell you that you need to get out and fast. You should never feel that you're trapped in a position. That is no way to live your life. Instead, you should think of where you can go and not let fear get in your way. It's the only way forward.

YOU'RE PHYSICALLY SUFFERING

You might be experiencing physical symptoms related to stress and job dissatisfaction. Your health might be suffering. In this case, your body might be telling you that this is not good for you and that you need to move on. Are you experiencing frequent headaches or feeling sick at work? Have that stomach pain that gnaws at you all day long, or find yourself going to the bathroom more than usual? Or, perhaps you arrive home and you feel a sudden wave of fatigue that makes you immediately crash on your couch or bed. Then, you think to yourself that you don't give a hoot about your job and that this will all blow over.

Other physical symptoms can include either weight gain or weight loss. Do you find yourself eating more or less than usual? Is your appetite changing because of stress, making you more vulnerable to health problems? Also, are you sleeping well at night or are you struggling to get some shut-eye, because you're stressed or nervous about the things going on around you?

What might be even worse is your constant feeling of anxiety and tenseness. You might also feel the anxiety working its way into your veins so that you literally cannot move a muscle and get out of your situation. That is a sign that things are not right and that you need a change as soon as possible.

POOR SELF-CONFIDENCE AND JEALOUSY

Because you're not feeling professionally challenged, you might feel that you're losing skills. Maybe you're backsliding with no way of getting out of it. Your everyday routine at work can quickly contribute to the loss of professional self-confidence, which can erode away at your self-image. This process results in a self-fulfilling prophecy: you believe you're not good enough, which means you're not even going to apply for a new job. This makes you feel even more stuck and less motivated to make a move out of your current position.

You have probably seen others around you who have spent a few years at the office and have used the opportunity to move up the career ladder. By looking around you, you might feel envious of others, who are constantly improving and moving forward, while you are staying right where you are and not budging. Jealousy and poor self-confidence are a recipe for failure and stagnation, which are not going to help you advance or get better at what you do. Instead, they will bring you down even further and not help you get back up. Don't put yourself in this position.

YOU ARE UNDERPAID AND UNDERVALUED

Another surefire sign it's time to move on is when your pay is affecting your everyday life and you're not getting any raises. The biggest sign that an employer doesn't value you is salary stagnation. You might feel you're giving 150% to your job, but you're only getting paid at 75%. Your employer might not have given you a raise or bonus in the past two years, and you want to get a raise as soon as possible. Furthermore, your boss might tell you the company is having economic problems and that everyone has to make a sacrifice. This is definitely a sign you need to move on. It's not worth spending time at a job where they don't value the time and energy you invest. Don't waste your effort on a job that is not going to royally reward you for your hard work. Being undervalued and underpaid is not the place where you want to be in your career. Move on as soon as possible and find a better paying position, one where your skills and experience are richly rewarded by your employer.

YOUR PERSONAL RELATIONSHIPS ARE SUFFERING

Another sign that it's time to go is that your personal relationships are suffering. This one goes beyond life at work. Your stress levels are making you an irritable person, and people can feel your stress and anxiety. This makes people not want to be around you as much. Because you spend so much time at the office and with your colleagues, you have no opportunity to bond with the people you love, including your friends, wife or husband, and kids. Since you're miserable in your professional life, you will also project those feelings in your personal life. Whenever you see that your relationship with your wife or husband is going down the tube, or that you have less time to spend with your kids and friends, you know that life at the office is taking its toll and you need to take some stock of your professional life and figure out what you can do to fix your problems. That likely indicates it's time to go. You should really think these things through. Whenever you feel you're hitting a wall in your relationships, you should consider moving on from your current position and taking on a new one.

YOU HAVE ACHIEVED A PERFORMANCE PLATEAU

It is possible you're sitting at your desk at work and you're feeling a backsliding sensation, because you're not moving forward, merely staying put. Your performance has reached a peak and you cannot go any further. Although you were motivated last year or last month, you've achieved your limit and capacity. Now, you're struggling with self-motivation, and you just want to go to work so you can earn money and feed your family. This is another feeling of being stuck that makes you want to move on. But you're still not sure how to do it.

PROMOTION IS A DISTANT MEMORY

Furthermore, because your performance has peaked and you were a lot better at your job a couple years ago, you feel demotivated. You didn't get promoted. In spite of your effort, you were not rewarded richly for your hard work. Instead, you felt underappreciated and undervalued. No one recognized your work, so you feel a bit down about it. You may have gotten promoted last year or two years ago, but there are no signs that you're going to get promoted in the future. This leads to further stagnation and demotivation at work.

YOUR CAREER DOESN'T ALIGN WITH YOUR VALUES

In addition, your current career doesn't align with your priorities or values. You believed that things would go a certain way, but reality proved to be much different.

Alternatively, your values and goals changed, which means that the job is no longer aligned with them. Are you still working for a company that conflicts with your views? You feel like you're compromising on your beliefs at work, because the business ethics of your company are not sound, and it's troubling you. If you find yourself stuck and trying to think your way out of it, that might be a sign it's time to move on.

SUMMARY

Do not ignore the early warning signs that something is not quite right at work. You have to do something about it. Take action. Don't stay in your contemplative mood: you have to act now. It's time for you to stop procrastinating and making excuses. This is not going to allow you to get ahead in life. Instead, you have to do what you can to get ahead. Find your passion and something that gets you going in the morning. Do something that is going to get you out of your comfort zone. You won't regret it for an instant.

3

MY JOB SUCKS! WHAT CAREER IS RIGHT FOR ME?

What is the right career for me? That's the million-dollar question, isn't it? In your job search, you should start by striking a balance between finding a fulfilling career and something practical, a field that has the potential to grow in the future, that pays well, that is known for the provision of bonuses and additional perks. When you discover a job and field that gives you passion, you're bound to have positive outcomes, including a higher salary, the ability to work with a dynamic team, and opportunities for learning and growth. You might be searching for a certain job, but you're not really sure where to start. How about starting with some introspection? It should help you contemplate and consider what path to pursue.

BEGIN BY ASKING YOURSELF IMPORTANT QUESTIONS

When you begin your search, you should start out by reflecting and pondering over the following questions. Think long and hard about them and give yourself time to deeply consider them.

What Do You Enjoy Doing?

Think about the type of work that gives you joy. When you go to work, you are drawn to working because it gives you a sense of fulfillment and purpose. You don't even have to consider it to be work. It could be a hobby or side job that you just happen to love. Think about the things that give you a lot of energy, not take it away. What are the things that boost your self-esteem and give you a lot of potential for the future?

What Are You Naturally Good At?

Everyone has a skill or talent that they have mastered over time. As they develop it, they can use it for greater purposes than themselves. If you're good at math and calculations, you could go for a job that uses numbers, like accountant or tax advisor. If you're good at science, you could consider a job in the life sciences. There are many options that you might think about. Just think about the things that come easiest for you, tasks and jobs that you don't have to break your back trying to do because they come natural to you.

What Have You Always Wondered About Having as a Job?

Do you have any childhood dreams that you want to explore? Do you recall wanting to be a doctor or nurse when you were young and wanted to pursue that later on in your life? We all have a dream that we maintain from an early age. Sometimes, we follow through on it, but in most cases, we do something else. It's just human nature.

If You Could Trade Jobs With a Friend, Who Would That Be?

Imagine you have a friend. They are successful and you envy them. It makes you angry and resentful toward him or her, because they have their life put together. You, on the other hand, are still living with your parents, and you want to move out as soon as possible. Consider your peers and where they are career-wise. Don't be envious of them; just think of where you might be. It's possible that you could be in their shoes in the future.

The Things You Hate the Most About Your Current Job Are...

Make a list of all the things that drive you up the wall

about your current job. What are the things that tick you off every day about it? What are the aspects that make you cringe and want to pack up and leave as soon as possible? Consider the early warning signs we have mentioned and add to them, if you can. Write everything down in your journal or on a piece of paper and stick it on your mirror in your room. Look at it and consider what you're going to do about it and contemplate your action plan.

The Things That You Are Missing in Your Current Job...

Now, make a list of all the things you lack in your current job that you want in a future position. What are the things that are going to make your life better with your current job? Is it the pay? The benefits? Another company that has better camaraderie and chemistry among coworkers? What about the atmosphere of your workplace? Write down everything you think is important for you to have in a future position and what will make you the happiest in your desired workplace.

What Do You Want to Be Known for When You Retire?

Next, think about what you want to be known for when you retire and leave the field. What lasting contributions to your field do you want others to know you have made? Will you have written books or articles that contribute to your community or niche? Do you want to build a legacy that will continue on after you've retired or even died? Consider the possibilities for the future and where your career may be leading you when you're finished.

If You Could Go Back to School, What Major Would You Choose?

Imagine going back to college and doing things over. More than a few of us regret what major we chose. Maybe we chose something like sociology, communication, or psychology, and we feel bad about it. Our only job choice seems to be customer service with JCPenney or another store at the mall. With our dead-end jobs and a lot of debt, we find ourselves without any choices. Sound familiar? Maybe you feel that way. Think about your ideal major, the one you would choose if you could do things all over again, change your major to a more profitable and rewarding one. It's okay to regret what you've done, but don't let that stop you from moving forward and changing things about your current situation. Your mindset is everything, and it can be what puts you back in the game.

DO A PROFESSIONAL SELF-ASSESSMENT

Now, think about your professional profile. What are your qualifications and the experience that have prepared you for a job in your chosen field? In some cases, there are a wide range of qualifications and backgrounds for job candidates, but you have to be honest with yourself. Where are you on the professional scale, and what is going to qualify you for the job that you want? It is important to ask yourself the following questions:

What Degree Do You Hold?

The first question you need to understand for yourself is what level of education you have, what degree you hold, and how that can help you in the job marketplace. Think about where you got the degree. Names can add value to your degree, especially if you graduated from a renowned university. Also, think about any coursework you took in college that has prepared you uniquely to take on the responsibilities of your ideal job.

Did You Go Through Additional Qualifications and Training to Boost Your Professional Skills?

If your degree was not helpful in getting you qualified, did you do further training to boost your resume? Did you do a certificate program online or get unpaid internship experience? Did you do pro bono or volunteer work that helped you get your feet wet in your chosen field? Write down all the experience you have attained that is relevant to the type of job that you intend to apply for. Make the list specific to the job you're envisioning.

What Set of Soft Skills Do You Have?

Now, think about what set of soft skills you have. What are the transferable skills you acquired in your current job that you could easily add to your repertoire at another company? Maybe that's communication skills or interpersonal relationship skills, or management or admin skills. There are many possibilities.

What Languages Do You Know?

Do you have language skills that would be useful in your field of interest? Can you speak Mandarin, Spanish, or any other useful, in demand language? Consider it an asset, add it to your resume, and think of ways you can use this skill in your career.

Based on the above information, you can easily determine if you're missing some important skills and whether you should undergo some training before pursuing a new career. The next step in this process is brainstorming.

DO A BRAINSTORMING SESSION

Now that you have collected some vital information, you can think about how your career has evolved and where you see it going. Sit down and do a brain-storming session about your career and current plans. Answer the following important questions.

Write About Specific Career Situations or Challenges That You Have Mastered

Did you complete a project that was difficult and required a lot of manpower and resources? Did you work successfully on projects, perhaps using project management methodology? Have you overcome any major hurdles or adversity that could have made you stumble? Write these down in your notebook.

What Approaches Have You Employed to Handle Challenges?

Write down the approach you have taken to handle challenges and adversity. Is there a specific method or mindset you have utilized to overcome difficulties that have come your way? Write everything in your journal or notebook.

What Was the Outcome of Your Situation?

Write down what the outcome was of your problem or situation. Did it all resolve itself successfully? Were there further hindrances that prevented you from advancing? Reflect on all the things that happened to you.

Do You See Some Kind of Trend or Pattern?

Ask yourself: "Do I see some kind of trend or pattern in all these situations? Do I act or behave a certain way in situations with a similar pattern every time?" Are your behavior and your reactions predictable? Are there any ways you can modify your behavior? What are the biggest skills you consistently show, and what were the situations that you managed to diffuse and conquer?

Write Down Some Essential Personal Skills That You Have

Finally, write down the essential personal skills and capabilities that you've tested through time. They should be the ones to focus on when doing your job search.

WRITE A LIST OF FUTURE CAREER PATHS

Having completed your self-assessment, you will probably have multiple lists of potential occupations available to you. To keep yourself organized, compile all of them into one list.

Try to find careers that appear on several lists and then put them on a blank page in your journal. Give this page a title like "Occupations to Consider." Your self-assessment will have shown that these occupations would be suitable for you based on your attributes and traits, so you should explore them.

Find the occupations on your lists that you want to consider. These careers may be jobs that you know a little bit about and you want to continue to explore. You might also think about careers you've not heard about much before. You could learn something in this process (McKay, 2019).

Narrow Down Your List

Having considered all the available options, you'll be happy to have narrowed down your list to only 15-20 options. You can now proceed to gather basic information about each of these options.

Find Degree Requirements and Job Descriptions

Use your research skills to find the job requirements for basic functions, as well as educational training expectations. Also, find out any licensing requirements in the sources that you search. Try to find out ways you can advance your career. One potential source of this information is government-compiled labor market information, which provides data about your job outlook and salary expectations (McKay, 2019).

"Short-list" It

With all this information, you can now narrow down

your list even more. Start crossing out careers that you don't think are right for you. You should have at most five occupations on this "short-list." If you think that a career is not suitable or if you have concerns about it, take it off your list. Don't include any careers that do not appeal to you. Cross off careers that have weak career outlooks. Eliminate any choice that has educational requirements or training that don't fit your current qualifications (McKay, 2019).

Add Information About Industry Forecasts for Each Field

Is your field of interest growing? Are there new jobs being added every year? Include information about the earnings potential as well as the new opportunities that are becoming available in your chosen field.

Add Information About the Pros and Cons of the Jobs on Your Short List

With your short list ready, you can now evaluate all the options on the list. Write out the pros and cons of each one of them. Critically evaluate them and consider the benefits and drawbacks of pursuing all the careers. Be honest with yourself and think about whether the benefits outweigh the downsides. You don't want to get into a career that has a lot of disadvantages. Think about all the positive sides to it, including workplace environment, independence, working in a team, salary, etc. And consider the possibilities of negative experiences, including high stress workplaces, lots of responsibilities, and other factors that might influence your decision (McKay, 2019).

Conduct In-Person Interviews With People in Your Field

For each of your short-list options, you can now do some more in-depth research. Conduct informational interviews with people who work in your field of interest. People who work in that field can give you firsthand knowledge and experience that can provide you with vital information about day to day activities and expectations of the career choice. You can find people through professional social networks, like LinkedIn. Or, you can also make use of the alumni network at your university or college, which would certainly be able to provide career guidance and advice.

Make Your Choice

After you have completed your research, you're ready to make a choice. Choose the career that will give you a lot of satisfaction and joy from the list that you have gathered. Recognize that it is possible you might want to reconsider somewhere down the road and that this is totally normal. Most people change their career multiple times, so be kind with yourself and accept that it may take a while to find the right career for you. This is a part of everyone's experience when just starting out (McKay, 2019).

MAKE A CAREER ACTION PLAN

The last step in your brainstorming process is action planning. Making an action plan is an important part of helping you reach your goals. Maybe you had a lot of career plans that you developed when you were studying or at other times. For you to achieve your goals, you need to create a concrete action plan, which will help you have a stronger vision for what you want to accomplish. You can use an action plan at any point in your career. Planning for your career is going to make your goals a reality and it will also help you prepare for a potential start in a new career if you are halfway through your professional journey. Here below, we have provided a concrete example for you to follow for a career action plan: use it to guide you. We will also provide a blank template for you to fill in after you have read the sample.

CAREER ACTION PLAN: SAMPLE

This career action plan is going to help you focus on your goals and plans for the future. It will help you work out how you are going to achieve what you want in work and life, and it will let you apply your knowledge and skills to successfully move into your next career.

Name: John Smith

Date: 17 March 2020

My Profile

Personal Characteristics

My current skills and abilities (Things that I do well, e.g: listening, problem-solving, or teamwork): I am a good team player and I work well independently. I provide counsel and advice to my coworkers and have a helpful demeanor. In addition, I know how to troubleshoot, and identify and resolve problems.

My Values (things that are important to me; e.g; honest and hardworking): I value a sense of camaraderie in a team. I want to do my best for my company and provide high quality and honest work to my team. I want to be dependable and respectful toward others and always commit myself to my promises. Integrity and hard work are important attributes to me.

My Interests: I am interested in psychology, music, therapy, social skills, emotional intelligence, among other topics. I also want to understand how people think and reason and relate to one another.

My Proudest Achievement: My proudest achievement was winning an award as Best in Delegation at a Model United Nations conference when I was in high school. As a shy and introverted student, I felt that I stood out at that conference and overcame my fear of public speaking. It was a wonderful time for me that I think has led me to become more people-oriented in my current work.

Self-Assessment Instruments: I have used a variety of self-assessment tools online including an online inventory, 16 Personalities, and other tests that have helped me develop a sense of what my interests are and how those can be used in a potential career.

Educational Background

Degree: I obtained my bachelor's degree in psychology from Boston University in 2010, and I got my therapist license in 2014, which enabled me to do online therapy and other psychotherapy sessions with patients.

Coursework: I have taken courses in psychology, therapy, liberal arts subjects, and others which are relevant to my interest in doing social work.

Completed certificates: I was awarded a certificate in advanced psychotherapy, which I have been able to use as a therapist for mental health clinics: the course has helped me be more in-tune with the various needs of my patients.

My Preferred Learning and Working Style: I prefer to learn by reading books, having conversations with people, and spending time thinking and reflecting. I like one-to-one conversations with people and prefer not to interact with groups of three or more.

Employment and Volunteer Achievements

Employer/Organization Name: Vision Therapy and Associates

Role: Psychotherapist

Duration of Work: 3 years

Tasks undertaken: I worked as a psychotherapist for Vision and Therapy for 3 years and worked with hundreds of patients providing them with group and individual therapy sessions on a wide variety of mental health topics, including addiction, depression, anxiety, among others.

Employer/Organization Name: Empathy Therapy Company

Role: Psychotherapist

Duration of Work: 2 years

Tasks undertaken: I worked as a therapist for Empathy Therapy Company for two years and provided therapy to a wide variety of patients who were dealing with trauma and other mental health conditions.

Community Involvement (Volunteering)

Organization Name: Big Brother and Sisters of Boston

Duration of involvement: 2 years

Tasks undertaken: I worked with the Big Brother and Sisters organization in Boston to provide mentoring and one to one support for boys who were struggling in school and did some tutoring sessions with them, which encouraged them to try their best.

My Future

How much do you already know about different options for education and training? You can try to explore different training options for the career choice of your future.

My Career Choice

Choice: Social Worker

Qualities Required (Check: www.myfuture.edu.au for more information): Excellent written and communication skills, good listening skills, willingness to work with patients for an extended period of time, patience, hard work

Duties: The ability to be on-call for patients, especially those in distress, communication with patients during different times, visiting the homes and schools of patients who are dealing with various difficulties.

Potential Employers: The local and state governments, social work companies, etc.

Employer Important Dates: January 10 and December 15: Testing dates for the National Psychotherapy tests

Employment Outlook: The field is expected to grow by 18% between 2018 to 2028 according to the US Bureau of Labor Statistics.

Education and Training Required: A degree in social work and a license in social work; candidates might also have other clinical experience in other fields, such as psychology.

Providers Offering Course: Training is provided at local universities and community colleges.

Course Requirements: Courses in social work or psychology would be appropriate to this field of study.

My Plan

Goals I Achieved Last Year: Last year, I was able to complete an advanced course in psychotherapy, which prepared me for a future of becoming a therapist and social worker. I also read 100 books over the course of one year, which is a goal I set for myself.

What I Have Learned About My Goal Setting Skills: I have learned that setting and reaching goals is a discipline that requires utmost dedication and hard work. It's not something you master overnight, and you just have to keep yourself going and never stop improving yourself. Always grow and learn new things.

New Education and Training Goals:

What is my goal? My goal is to become a social worker for the local government in Boston.

How will I do it? I will take courses in social work and apply to get my license in social work, which will help me start my career.

Why is it important? It's important for me to make this career change, because I want to help people who are in disadvantaged and impoverished situations to flourish and make meaningful contributions to society.

When will I do it? I want to make this career start by early next year in January.

Resources I Need to Help Me: U.S. Bureau of Labor Statistics, Learn How to Become.org, socialworkguide.org, socialworklicensemap.com

Who Can Help Me: My friends and family, professors, and mentors can help me reach my goals.

Areas I Need to Develop to Achieve My Career Choice

Attributes: I need to develop my interpersonal skills and communication skills so I can become more friendly and approachable. My goal is to approach new people in the next few weeks.

Achievement Deadline: Next month

Skills: I want to develop my academic skills in social work and learn many new things that will help me to get a job in this field. I need to complete my courses and build relationships with my fellow classmates.

Achievement Deadline: At the end of this month

My Review: During the year, you should find yourself reflecting on your goals and whether or not you have met the deadlines you set for yourself. Think about what it has been like to plan ahead and move successfully into your new career. As you reflect, you will see where you have grown and where you still need to go.

Which Goals Have I Achieved At This Stage?

My Educational and Training Goals: Last month, I completed my first semester of courses in social work, which will help me prepare to apply for a license in social work at the end of this year.

When I achieved them: Last month

My Employment Goal: My goal is to start applying for a job in social work next January and spend a month or two interviewing and then land the job after that time. I am also planning on getting a part-time job at Starbucks to make ends meet for the time in between job searching.

When I Will Achieve Them: Next January

Which Goals Need Further Work?

Goal: I still need to develop my relationships with my classmates in the courses I am taking on social work. I am still shy and reluctant to engage with them, so I want to break out of my shell and contribute to class discussions more actively.

People and Resources to Help Me: I'm going to ask my friends and family to help me with this piece.

Below, you can find a blank copy for your reference, if you want to fill in your own personal career action plan.

CAREER ACTION PLAN: TEMPLATE

Name: _____

Date: _____

This career action plan is going to help you focus on your goals and plans for the future. It will help you work out how you are going to achieve what you want in work and life. This career action play will let you apply your knowledge and skills to successfully move into your next career.

My Profile

Personal Characteristics:

My current skills and abilities:

My Values (things that are important to me; e.g; honesty and hard work):

My Interests:

My Proudest Achievement:

Self-Assessment Instruments:

Educational Background:

Coursework Taken:

Completed certificates:

My Preferred Learning and Working Style:

Employment and Volunteer Achievements

Employer/Organization Name:

1.

Role:

Duration of Work:

Tasks undertaken:

Employer/Organization Name:

2.

Role:

Duration of Work:

Tasks undertaken:

Community Involvement (Volunteering)

Organization Name:

Duration of involvement:

Tasks undertaken:

My Future

How much do you already know about different options for education and training? Try to explore different training options for the career choice of your future.

My Career Choice

Choice:

Qualities Required:

Duties Required:

Potential Employers:

Employer Important Dates:

Education and Training Required:

Providers Offering Courses:

Course Requirements:

My Plan

Goals are the things that you want to achieve in the future. These are the aspects of your life that will prepare you for changes in your work life. It is important for you to think about your individual goals, because then you can work out how you want to achieve them. Considering your goals is going to help you prepare your training, a list of the occupations that are a good fit for you, as well as keep your future options open. If you meet a goal during the year, set another one for yourself, perhaps a more difficult one.

Goals I Achieved Last Year:

What I Have Learned About My Goal Setting Skills:

New Education and Training Goals

What is my goal?

How will I achieve it?

Why is it important?

When will I achieve it by?

I want to make this career start by

——————————————

Resources I Need to Help Me:

Who Can Help Me:

Areas I Need to Develop to Achieve My Career Choice

Attributes:

Achievement Deadline:

Skills:

Achievement Deadline:

My Review:

Which Goals Have I Achieved at This Stage?

My Educational and Training Goals:

When I achieved them:

My Employment Goal:

When I Will Achieve Them:

Which Goals Need Further Work?

Goal:

People and Resources to Help Me:

4

THINKING ABOUT THE JOBS OF THE FUTURE

Pursuing one's dream is obviously the most important thing when it comes to getting unstuck. Some dreams, however, don't really have the potential to be transformed into profitable jobs. Apart from exploring personal passions, an individual should also go through some practical considerations when examining professional opportunities. Analyzing trends for the future and jobs that are likely to be in high demand can help for the creation of a professional shortlist filled with jobs that are both satisfactory and profitable.

We live in a rapidly changing world. As a result, some jobs become obsolete while the demand for others is growing. Let's look at a list of jobs that continue to require more workers during the coming decade.

THE 10 FASTEST GROWING JOBS FOR THE COMING DECADE (LIU, 2019)

According to the U.S. Bureau of Labor Statistics, there are many fields that are expecting to grow in the decade between 2018-2028 (U.S. Bureau of Labor Statistics, 2019). The labor force is expected to have marked increases in industry employment, which will grow at an annual rate of 0.5% (U.S. Bureau of Labor Statistics, 2019). The service industry will also grow at a rate of 0.5%. Consequently, there will be 7.6 million jobs added to the economy (U.S. Bureau of Labor Statistics, 2019). The result is that there will be 136.8 million jobs in the service sector. Areas that will experience the most growth will be private educational sector, healthcare, and construction work.

1. Solar Panel Installation Professionals

Projected Growth: This field is expected to grow by 63% in the coming decade.

Average Salary: $42,700

2. Wind Turbine Service Provision and Tech Support

Projected Growth: This field is expected to grow by 57% in the coming decade.

Average Salary: $54, 400

3. Home Health Aides

Projected Growth: This field is expected to grow by 37%.

Average Salary: $24,000

4. Personal Care Aides

Projected Growth: This field is expected to grow by 36%

Average Salary: $24,000

5. Occupational Therapy Assistants

Projected Growth: This field is expected to grow by 33% in the coming decade.

Average Salary: $60,000

6. Information Security Analysts

Projected Growth: This field is expected to grow by 32%.

Average salary: $98,000

7. Physician Assistants

Projected Growth: This field is expected to grow by 31%.

Average salary: $109,000

8. Statisticians

Projected Growth: This field is expected to grow by 31%.

Average salary: $88,000

9. Nurse Practitioners

Projected Growth: This field is expected to grow by 28%.

Average Salary: $107,000

10. Speech Language Pathologists

Projected Growth: This field is expected to grow by 27%

Average Salary: $78,000

JOBS THAT WILL BE DISAPPEARING

It's also important to have a good idea about some of the jobs that will be disappearing over the coming decade. According to Ibisworld, there are several industries that are fast declining:

- Sign & Banner Manufacturing Franchises. -21.2%
- Merchant Banking Services. -12.1%

- DVD, Game & Video Rental in the US. -12.0%
- Unmanned Aerial Vehicle (UAV) Manufacturing. -11.9%
- Apparel Knitting Mills in the US. -11.6%
- Postal Service in the US. -8.7% (Ibis Word, 2020)

It would be best to try to avoid focusing on these industries for future employment opportunities.

Although these are the main industries seeing the biggest decline, some service sectors and other occupations are seeing a decline in numbers, as well. Let's go through some of them.

Travel Agents

With websites such as Priceline, Expedia, Kayak, among numerous others, the need for travel agents has gradually declined over time. These websites are slowly reshaping an industry that used to be reliant on humans to discuss available destinations and sell various travel packages. Much of what you need to know about travel is now available freely on the Internet, therefore you don't need to consult a human to get the information. Plus, you can make reservations online for most parts of your trip, including airfare and hotels. Don't go for this type of job, because it may disappear completely within the next decade.

Bank Tellers

Bank tellers are becoming an obsolete profession. With the widespread use of ATMs that can do everything, including deposit checks and pay bills, you don't really need a person to help you get your banking operations done. In fact, you can do most if not all of your banking transactions online or even on your phone, because there are many apps available that tell you how to do anything you can imagine. Technology has become very advanced in the last several years. Consequently, the need for bank tellers will be non-existent in the near future.

Librarians

Gone are the days when the town librarian could direct you to all the resources you were looking for. These days, more people are learning how to Google and search for the information that they want for school, work, or any other thing. In the information age, all you have to do is go online, and there is a gold mine of resources waiting for you. Plus, if you want a book, you can check it out online and even read it before buying it on Amazon or any other bookstore on the Internet. Therefore, library science is a disappearing profession that may see far fewer opportunities in the future.

Telemarketers

Don't you hate it when telemarketers call you on the phone and try to sell you something? Well, don't worry about it too much, because pretty soon, these jobs will no longer exist. With automated services and digital advertising, calling people up on the phone and trying to sell them a product is becoming a less common phenomenon. Even if you were interested in this career, cross it off your list.

Postal Service Workers

The postal industry is one of the fastest disappearing professions, because of carriers, such as UPS and FedEx, which have expedited services for customers. Additionally, more people are relying on digital products, which do not require shipping and handling. With increasing amounts of automation and digital software, the postal industry will likely have fewer positions open in the future and may disappear altogether.

Typists and Word Processors

Between 2010 and 2020, the number of working word processors and typists decreased from 115,000 to 102,000. The 13,000 jobs that have disappeared can be explained by the fact that computers and automation are making it a lot easier for people to type without needing professionals to do it for them. Also, human typists have a margin of error that can be eliminated with the use of a machine typist, which can do the job much more accurately. If you're looking to expand your range as a typist and think you can land a good job doing it, quit while you're ahead and look for another profession that can use your skills, which is just about any desk job.

Electronic Equipment Assembly Professionals

Many electronics professionals are operating from automated sources. Robots are becoming the agents of assembly. With assembly lines and other streamlined processes, the electronic industry will become more machine-controlled, which will reduce the need for human management.

File Clerks

Again, with more things going online and AI becoming a widespread phenomenon, more of the work that is menial and administrative is being done online, and it makes it easier for machines to do the work, because accuracy is increased with computers and robots that have the capabilities of delivering quality work in half the time it takes for humans to complete the same task.

Florists

Between 2010 and 2020, the number of florists has decreased by 6,000 or almost 9.3%. The demand for flowers seems to be decreasing with time, and also with plant life becoming increasingly endangered by climate change, it is becoming harder for florists to make money.

Petroleum Pump System Operators

If you think you can get a job at any gas station, you will find that the demand is decreasing these days. Because automated and self-serve gas stations are becoming increasingly popular, having pump system operators is becoming unnecessary. Therefore, this career option is not going to be promising in the foreseeable future.

FUTURE-PROOF YOUR CAREER

It is important to future-proof your career if you're going to make a radical change right now. Today's economy necessitates a wide variety of skills and it will definitely continue doing so in the years to come. Think about your personal strengths, how they align with profitable industries and what would bring you professional satisfaction. This would likely be a goal that is much more important than earning a high salary.

Be Aware of The News and The World Around You

These days, it is important to read the news and become aware of the economy and new developments and trends. A good understanding of the world can help you make the right personal choices. Plus, it helps to be more knowledgeable of your surroundings because then you can actively engage with others and relate to the world around you.

Consider the Role of Technology in the Workplace

Think about technology because it will continue to affect most professional fields, with some technology eventually replacing human workers, as discussed above. With the invention and everyday use of artificial intelligence and robots, machines are being used instead of humans to operate many technical devices. The need to learn how to operate new technologies is becoming increasingly important for the workplace. Acquiring such skill right now can easily turn you into a field pioneer with excellent job prospects. Don't hesitate to get training now, increase your knowledge and enhance your skills. You never know when your technological prowess could come in handy in today's economy. It could very well land you in a job that will make an impact on this world.

CONCLUSION

There are many jobs out there that are going to become extinct and you don't want to be going down with a sinking ship. It is also crucial to find meaningful and well-paid jobs that are going to reward you for your hard work and dedication. It is not too late to look for a new job in another field. Many people find themselves leaving a field they have been in for a long time and yet, because of circumstances and industry changes, they have had to move on. There are many careers that will continue to grow in the next decade or two and you would do well to research those careers to consider if they might be a good choice and fit for your life. The use of technology and online workspaces is becoming more popular as they are proven to operate at higher levels of productivity. Recent worldwide events are helping drive that understanding in the marketplace as well. Find a career that fits your skills and passions and it will help you build a profession that is going to serve you. To help you with that, I have written *The Career of Consequence: Finding What Serves You* in the *Own Your Career* series as well.

5

PURSUING YOUR PASSION WHILE STILL MAKING A LIVING

Very few people will quit their current job before they've found a new one. The soundest strategy would be to continue working until something better is secured. Navigating through a full-time job and interviews, however, can stretch you to the limit. This chapter will provide you with coping strategies and practical tips you can employ while working and pursuing your dream career at the same time.

Are you looking to quit your day job and start something new? Perhaps you dream of starting your own business, or you might be looking into prestigious jobs that require multiple rounds of interviews and a lot of red tape. You might think that looking for a new job itself requires a full-time commitment in itself.

However, you should hold your horses right there. You need to think about some things first.

For a start, you need to decide if it is possible to quit your current job before securing a new one. Let's look at some factors you need to consider in your life.

FACTORS TO CONSIDER WHEN JOB-HUNTING

Examine Your Savings

Look at your savings account. Do you have enough money that can cover all of your living expenses for at least three months? Many people in this world live paycheck-to-paycheck, and it's not advisable to start something new unless you have the funds to help support you in the near future. Take a good look at your budget, what you can handle at this time and what you'll be able to do in the future. If you don't have enough to survive while you're without work for a few months, then you likely won't be able to make it. Be cautious and considerate of this point.

Take A Look at Your Schedule

Take a good look at your working hours. If you have a very rigorous schedule, it may be impossible to attend interviews while still keeping your job. It is important for you to be available to fly out to interviews, whether they are in your state or out of the country. Having that kind of flexibility will be an important consideration also for the type of jobs that you may be able to land.

Consider Your Support Network

Do you have a good support network (family, significant other) that can help you make the transition without experiencing financial strain? Your parents or relatives will become an important part of the equation. Are you confident in asking them for help, or do you find it to be a burdensome task you don't want to bother them with? Consider your relationships with your loved ones and how they may be impacted by your next career move.

Ask for a Leave of Absence or Reduce Your Schedule

Think about the possibility of asking for a leave of absence. Or, to make things a bit better, you could reduce your schedule. For example, you could move from full-time to part-time, or ask to have tasks shifted around on your schedule, which will make things more flexible for you. However, if you have no option to do this, then it might be better to quit your job altogether.

Quit if You Need Professional Qualifications

It's also a good idea to quit if you're going to need time

to attend courses and participate in professional qualification learning opportunities.

Now that you've answered these questions, are you looking to quit your job? It may be an option to look into after further consideration. Let's see how that can be done seamlessly and gracefully.

STEPS TO QUITTING YOUR JOB

Don't Feel You Need to Be Ready to Quit: Just Do It

Often, we might find that quitting our job is one of the scariest things we could do. If we're giving up a decent salary with benefits, we might consider it to be something we could never do. Most people don't have the guts to do it, which is why many people stay in jobs that don't provide meaning or fulfilment to them because they are too afraid to quit. However, you have to realize that life is short. We cannot go about our lives moping about, stressing ourselves to the max, doing jobs that only robots can do these days, and putting ourselves and our health in jeopardy. Therefore, you shouldn't feel you need to be ready to quit. Jump ship now; it's time to do it.

But Don't Be Too Impulsive About It

That being said, you have to have a plan. You can't just

walk into the office, have a temper tantrum, and quit the next day. That's definitely not the way to do it. You have to come up with your own reasons for quitting, and that should include a proper plan, for example starting your own business. You also have to psychologically prepare yourself for the process of leaving a stable, well-paying job for a path of uncertainty that might not even give you income for a year or two, or even longer. Before heading out the back door, you need to do a bit of self-reflection and make sure that you are not just having a bad day or a hard week. You need to be sure this is the right course of action for you, you need to have an action plan that you're willing to execute, and a strategy that, if executed properly, will get you where you want to be.

Avoid Burning Bridges

Many people usually give a two-week notice before they change jobs. However, often, it is better to give a lot more notice. Two or three months would be a very nice thing to do for your current employer, so they can take their time finding the right person to replace you. Maintaining ties with your current employer will be an important aspect of keeping your legacy strong, and reflecting a good professional image. Although you might not ever go back there looking to be rehired, it's always good to have positive referees who can vouch for you whenever you're looking for a new job.

Ignore the Old Adage: Have Another Job Lined Up

Conventional wisdom says that you need to have another job lined up before you quit your current job. However, Rosser has said that this is not a good idea. He said that if you take a sabbatical from your current line of work you can become a lot more successful in a future career.

Don't Think Too Much About It - Go for It

Often, we hesitate about quitting because we think too much about the consequences and the unknown, especially when we have to live off savings for a couple months. However, it is a good idea to prepare for it.

Prepare Financially for Your Move

Having your finances in order before you quit enables you to prepare to start your own business. Once you have a mortgage, car payments, student loan payments out of your life, you will be able to prepare for a future out of the workforce. In addition, if you have at least a couple years' savings in your back pocket, you will be able to handle the financial demands of quitting your job (Huddleston, 2019). The best thing you can do is live on a budget and continue to do that. Then, put money aside every month that you can save.

Automatically Transfer Money to Your Savings Account

It is important to get on the automatic transfers to your savings account as soon as possible. You need to start saving your money and putting even more money aside every month. Challenge yourself to add more to your savings every month, and get rid of the debts that often accumulate over time (Huddleston, 2019). Create a savings fund that is going to allow you to set aside a good portion of your income before you quit. Aim for 20-30% of your current income as a fund that you can access at any time, when you need it.

Explain to Your Boss What's Going On

Before deciding to quit, you should have a good discussion with your boss about what's going on. Maybe you're dissatisfied with the working conditions, the job functions, your salary, or new tasks, among many other things. It is important for you to lay things out in front of your current supervisor, because that also decreases the chance that you would burn bridges with your current employer (Huddleston, 2019).

Make Sure You Can Go Back to the Field

Having considered your options, notified your boss,

and prepared financially, you should also be prepared for re-entering your field after an absence. Perhaps you're considering taking a year off to travel the world or do something brave and adventurous. All things considered, you should have an action plan that will enable you to safely and securely go back into your field after you are absent for a while if you're out of the workforce due to job searching or taking a sabbatical from work.

Don't Jump Ship Before You're Ready

Maybe you've decided to quit, only to realize the job you had lined up failed to materialize. Maybe you just regret your decision. It can be an incredibly embarrassing thing to do, asking for your job back, but it happens to many people. Don't make the mistake of quitting before you're ready and you feel secure about your future. Not only can it be a costly mistake, but it can also result in professional embarrassment to you.

Be Aware of Your Reasons for Leaving

Before you decide to quit, you should be transparent with yourself as to why you want to leave your current job. Consider if it is your colleagues, your boss, the company, or the actual work that is making you want to pack your bags and get out of dodge. Think about whether the decision to leave will actually contribute to improving your life, or if you will live to regret it.

Don't Make Any More Excuses

If you think it's time to move on, you shouldn't procrastinate or make any more excuses. Although you might not have the biggest safety net available, you can still do things to increase your revenue, for example take on some side jobs, which should help you. You will always have excuses that you can make, and life is uncertain, but trying to shield yourself from that kind of vulnerability and uncertainty is not going to make you happier or more fulfilled at work.

With a Small Safety Net, You Can Go Forward

Maybe you don't have a large safety net and you feel that you will be at a financial disadvantage going forward. However, if you're going into a situation where you're starting your own business for the first time, you might find that not knowing where your next check will come from can propel you to achieve greater things with your life and career (Huddleston, 2019). You'll be filled with excitement, and while you might be living on your savings for a few months, you'll experience the joy of making bank when it happens. And eventually, things will start to stabilize. You just have to hold on and enjoy the roller coaster ride for what it is.

Believe That Finding A New Job Is in the Cards for You

Finally, you should have faith that finding a new job is going to be in the cards for you, and that you can find a new job at will. It can be an incredibly scary thing to leave one job to find another, but it can also be one of the most adventurous and advantageous things for your career and your life. You might quit and think that everything is going to hell. But what's the worst thing that can happen? You might have to work for a temp agency, at a coffee shop, or do retail work for several months. Keep your faith strong. You will be able to find a job in the future. The more time on your hands, the better. You will be able to apply for jobs passionately and with less stress.

THE SELF-EXAMINATION ROOM: 10 QUESTIONS TO ASK YOURSELF BEFORE YOU QUIT

Now that we've looked at some steps to quitting, we should also tell you more about the self-examination process that you might be wondering about. What should you think about before you quit? What are some questions you should be asking yourself? In this section, you will find ten questions that you need to consider as you're making the decision to leave your current job.

1. Do You Have Flexible Time in Your Schedule?

Look at your timetable and the daily list of responsibilities that you have. Do you have an important job, and many people on your team who count on you? In this case, it might not be realistic to keep this job while you look for another one. You could certainly begin to prepare your job applications by sprucing up your resume, researching companies, and doing interview preparation. But all of this needs to happen in your own time, and if you're not getting enough time to do that, then you need to consider stepping down from your current position entirely (Ceniza-Levine, 2018).

2. Can You Remain Low Key and Confidential in the Process?

It is crucial for you to maintain a high degree of confidentiality in the job search process. But in some situations, you might find it difficult to do that, especially if you're in a small field where everyone knows everyone else. Are you answering phones during work hours or trying to schedule interviews during your break times? It might start to look suspicious and your boss might eventually ask you about it, in which case you would have to make it "hush-hush" or try to avoid the conversation altogether. In any case, it's obvious that keeping it a secret is a high priority, but if that is hard for you due to your position or your specific field, then quitting may be the best option for your job search (Ceniza-Levine, 2018).

3. Is There Someone in Your Company Who Can Help You?

It would be great if your boss was to be the most helpful and supportive person in your company. They would be able to contribute to your growing CV and provide you with a reference for a potential position higher-up in another company. That's an ideal world we're talking about, not necessarily the real one. In all likelihood, you might find yourself disgruntled because your boss is distant, unsupportive or even abusive, which means you would have no help from him or her. But do you have someone at your company you can confide in or ask for support? If you haven't connected with anyone in your company, and you can find no one who can vouch for you in a time of need, then it's time to move on.

4. Is There Another Role You Can Play in Your Current Company?

Sometimes what we're looking for is closer than we realize. For example, you might find that your current job function is not enticing, so you want to find something else. However, the greener pastures might just be within your own company. You might need to ask around about new positions that are opening up in other departments or with other functions in the same company. Moving up can also be a lateral move, so try to find something you can do in another department. You don't have to pack your briefcase and leave just yet. You might be able to grab the golden ticket that secures you the next great opportunity right in your own back-yard (Ceniza-Levine, 2018).

5. Can you talk to HR or Your Boss About Changes?

Sometimes, we need to have difficult conversations. It's not easy but we have to do it. Confronting people who are your superiors, including your boss or HR, is risky business, and you don't want to make mistakes in the process. However, if you gloss over having an impor-tant conversation with them, it could be costly to your future. Consider the possibility of someone helping you with whatever is ailing you at work. But if they are unsupportive, then see it as a sign that you need to leave.

6. Are You Feeling Negative Outside of Work?

If you're in a job you hate, you will likely be suffering the consequences not only in your professional life but also in your personal life. Is work taking a toll on your health and overall outlook on life? If you find yourself stressed, binge eating or drinking, or doing any other unhealthy activity, it might be the time to get out. You can create a much healthier outlook that will be helpful to you. Negativity is infectious and it will destroy your whole concept of yourself and your life. Don't let it take you down.

7. How Will You Take Care of Your Expenses for Up to Three Months?

Most people who work have financial obligations and bills to pay. It can take a while to apply for a job, grad school, or another training program. Having a minimum of three months of pay is important to have to prepare for that period where you won't be earning any money at all. Think about all your expenses and consider any alternate sources of income, like jobs that you can do on your weekends. Try to find a side hustle that floats your boat (Ceniza-Levine, 2018).

8. Can You Get a Leave of Absence or Severance Pay at Your Company?

Think of asking for a leave of absence or severance from your company. You might need some money at the end of your contract, or you could request sever-ance pay. Don't be afraid to ask this question to your boss. The worst thing they can do is say "no," but if they give you a "yes" for either request, then either take the time off offered, or say your goodbyes and get a paycheck to keep you afloat while you are job hunting.

9. Have You Planned What You Will Do with Your Time Off?

Often, we feel that we are limited to our time at the office and we cannot think clearly about our other options. But you need to be prepared to consider what you will do with your time off. How will you budget your expenses, keep track of your spending, and plan for your next steps? Every step is important.

10. Have You Considered Making Adjustments Outside of Your Professional Life?

The last area that needs to be considered is the possibility of making adjustments in your non-work life. That includes your relationships, money, health, and stress management. Before you change jobs, it is important for you to do self-care and help yourself manage the stressful aspects of job hunting and being without income for a while. You have to take care of yourself and provide yourself with a good foundation that will prepare you for the next phase of your life. By enhancing other aspects of your personal life, like getting into a relationship, starting up a hobby, getting hired for a side job, or many other pursuits, you will be well on your way to a new career that will bless you in all areas, not just in your professional life (Ceniza-Levine, 2018).

TIPS ON LOOKING FOR A JOB WHILE YOU'RE EMPLOYED

Not everyone is looking to quit their job tomorrow, and many people don't have the option or luxury to do this. If you are in this situation, then you need to consider how you can prepare your exit strategy in the most expedited manner. Here are some tips for doing that.

Negotiate Some Flexibility

If possible, you should negotiate some flexibility without letting your supervisor know what you need the time for. Suggest that you need to shift around your schedule for different reasons, but don't offer any hints as to what you're doing during your time off.

Don't "Out" Yourself

It can be a difficult thing to remain quiet and self-composed about your job search. You might want to be chatting with your colleagues about a bad interview experience, or you might want to talk about how you can't wait to get out of the office. Instead of wanting to let it all hang out, you should stop yourself. If you tell one colleague, you might as well be telling the whole lot of them.

Dropping hints extends to your social media interaction. It is likely that some of your colleagues or superiors will keep tabs on your social media usage, including Facebook and Twitter accounts. Therefore, you should be extremely cautious as to what you post, because if it is even closely related to a job interview or another part of the job-hunting process, it could jeopardize your current job. Don't say something like "Wish me luck for this interview," or vague updates like "something exciting is going to happen this week." Stop yourself before you go too far, and simply don't use social media as a place to give announcements that you are not ready to make yet.

Schedule Your Job Interviews Outside of Your Normal Working Schedule

You should be wise and considerate and try to schedule any job interviews outside of your normal work hours, because it will also help you avoid "outing" yourself as discussed above. You can only have so many 10am doctor appointments before you start to raise eyebrows and set tongues wagging about what you're doing on those days. Instead, think about scheduling your interview in the early morning, during lunch, or even after work hours. It's possible you might not be able to do this. If that is the case, then you should think about taking a personal or vacation day. You might think that you could call in sick; however, that is a risky option that you should avoid. Take a day off in which you won't have to work, and you will be able to focus 100% on the interview itself (Autenrieth, n.d.).

Don't Adopt the "Couldn't Care Less" Attitude

When you're getting ready to quit, you might develop an attitude of no longer caring about what you do at work. Just as long as you're out of there, baby. But you shouldn't have that kind of attitude, because it could be self-sabotaging. Don't try to get by doing things that wouldn't fly on a normal day. Don't go job searching using the company computer, or take phone calls about your job-hunting process at work. You risk losing your current job, which will not be helpful for you to secure a new job. Stay focused on the task at hand and stay professional at all times. Live each day, a day at a time, and don't engage in any funny business. It's just not worth it.

Make the Most of LinkedIn

Do make the most of your professional social media accounts, including LinkedIn, which allows you to post your resume online and lets you connect with potential employers and colleagues. Make sure you keep your profile up to date with relevant information about your professional life. It's as good a habit as keeping your resume up-to-date every day: you never know when a job opportunity could come your way if you use this method.

Don't Act Rash

Just because you scored an interview at an incredible company that offers a generous compensation package and excellent colleagues, it doesn't mean you have sealed the deal. You have to approach any interview with a grain of salt and a bit of humility. You never know how an interview is going to go. Remain calm and collected at all times.

Don't Include Current Contacts at the Office as References

It might be tempting for you to write down the names of your boss and colleagues on your application, but you should wait until the very end of the process. Reference checks usually occur at the very end of the job application process. You don't want to be premature and put your current boss down as a reference. If a potential employer happens to call your current employer before they decide on your application, you might surprise your current boss before you get the job

(Autenrieth, n.d.). And then, it could ruin the whole plan.

Maintain Good Ethics

In all situations, you should act ethically. It's not okay to badmouth your current employer, even if you're really frustrated and tired of your current job. You might feel tempted to let it all out and simply release all the tension that has been welling up inside of you for a long time. Save it for a trip to the therapist's office.

Be on Top of Things

Because you are working a full-time job and don't have the luxury of sitting at home all day applying to jobs, you have to manage your time and energy. You must stay focused on your tasks at work, but also look for new opportunities (Autenrieth, n.d.). It's vital for you to stay organized and plan accordingly. Continuously update your resume and LinkedIn profile and craft an excellent template for your cover letters, so you don't have to start from scratch every time you make an inquiry. Organize your time well and mark your calendar to avoid double-booking yourself.

Ask for Discretion

When it comes to hiring managers at other companies, you will find that they are aware of the fact that your current employer is unlikely to be in the loop about your job search. You should be clear about your expectations of discretion. If the person who is a prospective employer is not willing to honor your preferences, then you should find another workplace. Being careful is very important (Autenrieth, n.d.).

Avoid Acting Unwisely

In all situations, it is better safe than sorry. If you don't have a job lined up, don't say anything about it until you get the offer. You should watch every action or word you say to others. You need to walk with a gentle step through every part of the process. You might be dreaming of a job at that fantastic start-up, and you only see the greener grass over there, because here at your current dead-end job things are rough. But it is also possible you might find some reasons to stay in your current line of work. Sometimes the job search makes us appreciate aspects of our work that we didn't even see before. In some situations, it's better to stay than leave. It's up to you to decide how to proceed.

TO QUIT OR NOT TO QUIT, THAT IS THE QUESTION

Both approaches have their pros and cons. It can be helpful for you to quit your job and start over from scratch by focusing 100% on your job search. You will find that you have a lot of free time and you can focus on your health and wellness, and on your job search. The downside is that you will have no income going into your bank account, so you will likely need to have financial resources to keep you going for the duration of your hiatus from work.

On the other hand, looking for a job while you're employed is going to be helpful because you will still be working and making money. You will be able to pay your bills and not worry too much about your finances. By staying in a job you hate, however, you will be distracted and feel demotivated. With this low morale, you might be tempted to do things that could jeopardize your current job. You will also not have a lot of flexibility with your time to apply for jobs and attend interviews. It could get really stressful for you.

In the end, only you can decide if you're going to keep your current job or quit. Whatever you choose, don't put off the decision too long because you could eventually lose your courage and discontinue the quest for the perfect job.

6

GETTING FROM POINT A TO POINT B

The research has been done and the self-analysis process is finally complete. It's now time for you to begin undertaking the steps that will eventually help you to become unstuck from your current professional misery. This chapter is going to be the most extensive and most practical one, delivering step-by-step explanations and strategies for identifying your dream job and securing that position.

You've now done your research and you've gathered the courage to change your job. It's now time to embark on your career change journey. Let's look at ways you can get started.

INFORMATIONAL INTERVIEWS

Talk to people who have gone through a serious career change. These people will be your role models and sources of motivation. They will give you ideas and pointers as to what it takes to complete the shift successfully. Talk to them candidly about their likes and dislikes in the job. Ask them the following series of questions; they will help you get an idea of what to expect.

Can You Tell Me What Got You Interested in This Job or Career?

Give your interlocutor the chance to tell their story from their point of view. Maybe they could tell you about their career journey, including any ups and downs they had, listen to their stories as you may gain valuable insight.

Did You Expect You Would Be in This Career for Long?

This is a leading question from the first. You can ask about how long they were in this position and their original expectations for their career.

What Made You Switch Careers or Jobs?

Ask them honestly what made them consider a career change, and how they were able to make the switch.

What Do You Love Most About Your Current Job?

Ask them what they enjoy about their current position.

What Is A Typical Day in Your Life?

Have them describe a typical day in their life and what they would do at work.

Are There Any Responsibilities That Can Be Tedious or Frustrating?

You can candidly ask about anything that may be tedious or frustrating in this job.

What is the Process for Applying for This Position?

Ask about the job application process for this position specifically.

How Were You Hired?

Ask your interlocutor how they were hired and what the process was like in their unique situation.

Do You Have Any Advice About the Job Application Process?

Specifically ask your interlocutor about what could

help you in the process of getting hired for the job that you want.

Is There Anyone You Might Be Able to Introduce Me to Who Could Tell Me More?

The last question is a follow-up question that can lead your informational interview to next steps, including forming connections and obtaining contacts that could lead you to a job interview.

BUILD YOUR REPUTATION BOTH ONLINE AND OFFLINE

The next bit of advice is to build your reputation both online and offline. First, you need to create a stellar CV. Your CV is one of the most important aspects of your application, which is the first thing any employer will see from you. First impressions matter: you need to make the best impression you can to ensure that your application stands out. You don't want your CV to be tossed in the bin. Let us look at what an excellent creative and industry-relevant CV looks like.

SAMPLE CV

ISAAC RICHARDSON: ADDRESS: 166 NEWMAN STREET, BOSTON, MA 02108

Phone (617) 846-9425

Objective: *To provide technical support for an IT company in the Boston metropolitan region and to be a consultant in IT mobile technology*

Work Experience

IT Technician, The Fantastic Corporation, Startup, Boston, MA

Dates: 03/2019-02/2020

Responsibilities:

- Provided technical support to a new startup company in France
- Created websites for the organization and managed their development
- Managed a team of IT technicians
- Prepared data and information for regular reporting and data analysis
- Established operation strategies to improve sales
- Served as a member of the IT marketing team

IT Technician and General Manager, The Enigma Room, Startup, Newton, MA

Dates: 02/2018-02-2019

Responsibilities:

- Managed a small team of startup employees at The Enigma Room
- Provided extensive technical support to The Enigma Room employees
- Served as a resource person for other IT technicians
- Mentored a group of new members and initiated them to the team
- Created an IT library accessible to all members and clients of the organization
- Established operation strategies in a team for improving sales.

Education

Bachelor's Degree in Computer Science, Massachusetts Institute of Technology, Cambridge Massachusetts, 2018.

IT Technician Certification, Massachusetts Institute of Technology, Cambridge, Massachusetts, 2018.

Additional Skills

Microsoft Office: Microsoft Word, Excel, Access, Database Operation: Microsoft Access, C++, SQL, HTML, STATA, SPSS, among many others.

Other Competences

English: Native Speaker

Spanish: Advanced Proficiency in Speaking and Writing

French: Advanced Proficiency in Speaking and Writing

German: Elementary Proficiency in Speaking

Projects

Website Localization of The Cloud website in 2017. Translation of a website from English into Spanish and French.

Website Creation of The Creative Life website in 2018. The website used creative design and original content to attract new customers.

References

References are available on request.

Polish Your Social Media Profile

Often, we put something on social media and then we leave it to sit for a year or two. Instead of letting your social footprint collect dust, polish it and make it relevant to your current career trajectory: make sure to provide complete information about your experience and professional background.

Start A Blog or Personal Website

In the digital age, there are many ways to enhance your online presence and build a stellar reputation online. You can create a blog and a personal website that can act as an additional reputation establishment resource. You can talk about the things that you are passionate about, and you can share your ideas with a wider public. In fact, you can become an authority in your field just by posting regularly on your blog, which will increase your credibility and make you a more likeable and respectable person.

Connect with Industry Leaders and Influencers

Next, you should connect with the leaders of your industry and influencers in your field. You might feel that you don't have a lot to say to these people. But the more confidence you build, the more empowered you will feel to approach them. You might not be butting heads with them at the bar, or having coffee with them, but get to know them by connecting on LinkedIn or sending a courteous introductory email letting them know your interest in them and the field.

Attend Professional Development Workshops, Seminars, and Conferences

One of the best ways you can enhance your personal development is by attending workshops, seminars, and conferences. These activities enhance your CV and also provide you with opportunities to train and teach others about your interests and passions. If you attend a workshop or seminar, you will learn from the leaders in your field. If you happen to be in a position to present, you will become a person who can stand out to others and project a degree of authority and expertise on a topic, which could make you an attractive candidate for the industry you're trying to enter.

Engage Others in the Process

It's crucial that you find ways of engaging others in the process of changing jobs or careers. Don't try to do it alone. We all need each other to get into a certain field: we cannot rely solely on our will power. Indeed, there is power in numbers. When you connect with others, especially those on the inside, you will find that job opportunities abound. That is why you should consider networking. We will explain more about it in Chapter 7.

SAVE MONEY

We have already addressed this in a previous chapter, but it bears repeating: one of the most important things you need to do before embarking in a career change is save money. You should put a decent chunk of your hard-earned cash in a savings account. If you do not have good savings, switching careers can be difficult. If you have enough money on hand, you will be able to take care of yourself and of your family during your break from regular employment. Additionally, you can be more selective about what kind of gig you eventually want to land.

Savings allow you to quit your current job and focus entirely on your new professional quest. Savings also will make it easier to potentially launch your own business, if that's where you're headed.

CHANGE YOUR MINDSET

The growth mindset is one that enables professionals to achieve great things. It helps you focus on eliminating negative self-talk. If you have to, attend a couple interviews for jobs that you're not interested in. By following this advice, you will be able to build your confidence and perform well when you need to do your best.

CONTINUE SELF-DIRECTED LEARNING

You should aim to be a lifelong learner. Never stop at simply being a student at university. You should constantly be developing yourself and learning more about the world. Learn a new language, start a new hobby, or even join an online educational program. The more you learn, the more skills you will be able to add to your repertoire, which will enhance your performance both at your current job and in your future dream role.

SEEK VOLUNTEER OPPORTUNITIES

You may need to gain skills and experience in a field that you don't know anything about before you can get a job in that area. Instead of going straight into work at a company and facing a steep learning curve, why not try volunteering? You can give back to the community and find some more meaning to life. You can try your hand at a variety of different roles, but you don't have to change jobs to do it. Volunteering is not the same as having a real job; however, it can provide you with a real-world look at what it's like to work in a given industry on a day-to-day basis, which will be even more helpful than conducting an informational interview. Volunteering can also be considered just as valuable experience as actual paid work experience, as well (Ferguson, 2018).

FIND A COACH OR MENTOR

Finding a mentor or coach is an important part of the application process. You need to find someone who can support you through the ups and downs of this endeavor. You can also bounce ideas off them at any given time. Additionally, a mentor should be someone who strongly supports you and believes in you. You should try to find mentors among the people you already know, which will help you get ahead in your industry (Ferguson, 2018).

LEARN FROM YOUR MISTAKES

The process of finding a job will potentially lead you to have some negative experiences. You should use those as learning opportunities. Ask for some feedback after unsuccessful interviews. Evaluate what was missing and what you could have done better. We all make mistakes, and we need to learn from them. Allow yourself to grow from all the things you do and continue to challenge yourself. It is important to always be growing and never settling. Learn from the experience and use your learnings in your future job seeking efforts.

MAINTAIN YOUR WORK-LIFE BALANCE

During your transition period, you should maintain a good work-life balance. Don't go all work and no play during this time. You need your freedom and the ability to do all the things to keep you healthy and happy. Continue to do self-care exercises at home, which will greatly enhance your quality of life and make you healthier.

OCCUPY YOUR TIME: TRY FREELANCING PROJECTS

If you quit your job and you need to occupy yourself with something while searching for a new job, try free-lance projects. Who knows - you may actually discover a new career this way. This can happen as people discover the independence and freedom of freelancing and never want to go back to a 9-5 job. Often, it is in freelancing that we find we can earn some extra cash, while doing something productive and meaningful, thus benefiting from the entire process.

DO NOT GIVE UP!

It is important for you to not give up at any time in this process. Job searching can be discouraging and even soul-sucking at times. Often, it takes longer than we want it to take, which can be frustrating and exhausting. However, if you push through, you will find that your endurance and perseverance will pay off and you will find a career that suits your needs, experience, and interests. Believe in yourself and believe that you can get the job done, and that all the craziness and stress of job searching will all be over when you finally snag the job of your dreams. Rinse and repeat as many times as necessary.

SUMMARY

Getting from point A to point B can be challenging, especially when you have a lot of steps to take. Depending on your situation, you might be changing careers while already having a full-time job you need to still work at, or you might have to quit your job, in your quest for the ideal one. It takes a lot of patience, perseverance, and dedication to get to where you want to go.

However, once you change your mindset, you will be able to reach your destination. Continue pursuing self-directed learning opportunities, volunteering, professional development, and mentorship opportunities. All of these aspects of professional life will give you a boost both on your CV and with your overall outlook.

7

THE POWER OF NETWORKING

A strong and reliable professional network is a massive asset that should be nurtured and used to get unstuck and to pursue one's dream career. What are some of the networking essentials and how can you utilize your social circle to make a career change possible? Where should you seek opportunities, and should you be proactive, or just wait for chances to materialize out of thin air? Let's now look at the ways in which you can enhance your networking skills and increase your chances to land some solid job opportunities.

DON'T BURN BRIDGES

The first thing you need to do is not burn bridges. The fact that you're dissatisfied with your current job doesn't mean you should leave on bad terms. It's important to maintain a good relationship with people, even if you have had a negative work experience with them. This is fundamental regardless of what company you work for, because businesses know other businesses, and the world is small. Connections are everything when it comes to the job market, and oftentimes, someone you know knows someone else, and so on.

LET YOUR FRIENDS, FAMILY, AND COLLEAGUES KNOW

Because connections are essential to getting your next job, it is crucial to use your existing contacts to help you. Perhaps, your friends and family know someone who knows someone in a company, and then you could start the connection there. You never know how close you might be to landing a job, even by looking at your current network and others' as well (Zhang, n.d.).

DETERMINE THE TYPES OF STRATEGIC CONTACTS YOU SHOULD PRIORITIZE

Next, you should think about the types of strategic contacts you should put at the top of your list. You might include other professionals you have partnered up with through the years, or former coworkers, who may be now gainfully employed elsewhere or who have started their own business.

Coaches

Coaches are the type of people who motivate you and cheer you on. These are people who are on the sidelines helping you prepare your portfolio and your interview questions. If you let them, they will help you get where you want to be. They are not necessarily your close friends, but they can be people who will support you 100%, no matter where you want to go. Find this type of person to be a strong proponent of you (Ceniza-Levine, 2018).

Connectors

Connectors are the typical people-persons, who are heavily invested in others and know what's going on in their workplace and field (Ceniza-Levine, 2018). They know literally everyone and have built a reputation as social butterflies. Often, these people can become excellent resources for you, but you have to know how to approach them. They are often busy people, so you cannot expect that they will devote a lot of time and energy to you specifically. However, if you have specific questions in mind to ask them, you will likely be able to get some interesting and useful answers. But you also need to stay in touch with them and not take them off your radar.

Experts in Your Field

You should also get to know experts in your field. These people will know everyone who is an authority figure in your field, as well as all the companies and organizations that do the type of work you're interested in doing. Reach out to some experts in the field with specific questions you have and stay in touch with them. They might be an incredible resource to you (Ceniza-Levine, 2018).

Industry Leaders, Gurus, Mentors, and Influencers

Do your research on all the industry leaders and other people who are important in your field. Add them to your professional network on LinkedIn. If you can, hold informational interviews with them via phone or in person. Also, use this technique to find people who could potentially mentor you and provide you with information that will contribute to your success.

Academics in Your Field

Read up on all the relevant academic literature in your field. Get to know the academics by meeting them at conferences or other networking events. Do a presentation at a conference, or attend their session and ask them a lot of pertinent, smart questions. Offer to buy them coffee and have a small chat, which may allow you to find more information about your field of interest and their research scope.

The Alumni Network at Your Alma Mater

Your Alma Mater has a lot of resources you can tap into, which can help you find people, companies, and possibilities. By reaching out to and conducting informational interviews with the people you can find on the alumni website and resources, you will be well on your way to networking to a new job.

THE BEST NETWORKING STRATEGIES FOR YOUR CAREER CHANGE

Request Help from Your Network, but Don't Overdo It

When you're networking, you need to be thinking long-term and not just short-term. Additionally, you should not exploit the relationships that you have; instead, you should gradually build up your network over time with different contacts. Don't expect to ask for a job when you first meet someone. You should also not ask someone to put in a good word for you if you just met them at a conference or event. If and when you do need to ask for help from others, do it kindly and respectfully. Explain your situation (for example, you need a job now and would appreciate the advice) and kindly ask for help. Don't treat it as a one-sided deal. Instead, you should offer to return the favor in the future (Monster.co.uk, n.d.).

Be Attentive to Your Network

You need to be attentive to your network and how it is evolving. If you don't keep it intact, it may not serve its purpose once you need to use it. Furthermore, you need to be following up with people, communicating with them on social networks, introducing new members to your network, and always be prepared to give help to those in need. Try to remember people's names, as well as their interests and hobbies. "People persons" do this very well. They tend to have an encyclopedic brain of names, people, and their respective interests (Monster.co.uk, n.d.).

How to Tap into Your Network

Often, we don't want to admit that we need help. But you need to start somewhere, especially if you're looking for work and want to find a way of breaking into the field you want to enter. Let's look at ways you can begin your communications with people in your network.

1. Begin with a cordial greeting and then move on

   to your main point.

2. Explain in clear terms what you're asking their help for.

3. Give a narrative that highlights your motivations and goals, which provides a context for what you're talking about, but don't blow it out of proportion.

4. Provide all the information they need.

5. Give a deadline, if you need to mention it. (Monster.co.uk, n.d.)

Offer to return the favor if at all possible. And don't forget to thank them by sending a note or a greeting card. Shows of gratitude and appreciation go a long way, and it is a courtesy that you should show people who help you out.

Don't Just Ask for Information About Job Opportunities

When you're asking for advice, don't simply ask someone if a job is available at their company. People will see right through this and not offer you any help. You should be more attentive to the long-term possibilities of establishing a relationship with someone, and not simply asking about employment. Instead, you should ask your network for advice on how to advance your career. You could inquire about professional development opportunities being offered in your area.

Additionally, you could ask about potential training courses or education that is offered, which can greatly aid you in acquiring the skills and the knowledge needed to perform in your ideal job. Finally, you can receive mentorship and guidance from those who have been in the field much longer than you.

Attend Industry Events, Workshops, and Seminars

Networking events are important because they provide you with the best opportunities to meet other people in your chosen field. Attending a conference or seminar will offer you a chance to meet with different people who can provide you with a wealth of information and resources, and not just jobs! While you might think that going to a networking event will make it possible for you to ask employment-related questions, you should never attend just for that reason. Instead, you should use the opportunity to help you acquire knowledge and develop competence in your field. Learn from others who know more than you and take careful notes on what they're doing, as they present their ideas, research, and marketing plans. All of this can be fodder for your own ideas.

Organize Your Own Informal Events or Meetings

Take the initiative and organize your informal meetings or events with contacts on your list. This will give you the chance to meet people and have a conversation over coffee or lunch. You can also host your own networking events at your workplace or in an informal space. Personalize those meetings: there's nothing worse than showing someone that you don't know them well or that you don't remember how you met. For this reason, you may want to write down notes each time you meet someone new or interact with them.

SUMMARY

Networking is one of the most essential parts of your job search process. The sooner you can get on it and establish contacts with people in your field, the sooner you will have access to new career opportunities. Think of it all as a long-term process. You can't build contacts in a week and expect them to be able to help you with your job search. Any relationship requires time and dedication. You should make sure to be attentive to these relationships, and keep in touch with the people who may be in a position to help you in the future. Likewise, you should be willing to offer help and advice to other network contacts who might ask you to return the favor, as well. Use networking to your advantage, and you will be well on your way to the job of your dreams.

8

A NEW JOB OR A NEW BUSINESS

This final chapter will examine the possibility of starting your own business. Many people are already exploring opportunities like freelancing or launching a home-based company. Could that be the way forward for you? Can anyone launch their own business and be successful? Starting such an endeavor is one of the scariest prospects for most people, but more often than not, you have nothing to lose by trying.

Let's find out if you have what it takes.

HOW TO KNOW IT'S TIME TO QUIT YOUR JOB AND START YOUR OWN BUSINESS

You're Prepared but There's Not Enough Time on Your Hands

You may be working on your side job on the weekends or in the evenings, but if you want to turn your side hustle into a full-time job, you're going to need a lot more time than that. While juggling all the responsibilities of your day job, you will likely not have a lot of time and energy on your hands, which makes it impossible to do a lot of work outside of your working hours. If you come to a point where you just don't have enough time to devote to your business venture, it might be a sign that you need to quit your job and start your new business.

You Have the Managerial Knowledge and Industry Experience

Perhaps, you have worked in your industry for a long time, and you have built a wealth of experience that is needed to do your job well. You know all the ins and outs of the field, and you feel aware of what the job market is like out there. This will put you in an ideal position to take care of finances and all of the different responsibilities you will have when you become your own boss.

You Have a Well-Developed Business Plan

With your knowledge of the industry, you will also have a business plan which you have prepared to the finest detail. You will have created something that will help you flourish when you're on the market, and you know how to manage finances, tasks, and marketing strategies that will enable your business to take off.

You Have Sufficient Funding, or You Can Secure A Source of Funding

You need to ask yourself if you are financially prepared to start a new business. Before you start, you will need to have a good amount of cash to open up your business. This includes months of living expenses for yourself and your family, but you will also have to know how to budget so you can carefully track how you spend every dollar. Being intimately aware of your finances is an important part of being your own boss, because you will not only operate as your own manager but also as your accounting director, marketing manager, etc. You will have a great deal of responsibility, therefore, you need to be careful with how you spend your money and prepare well, because it's likely you won't be making much money in the beginning. Often, it takes a year or more for you to make a profit. In the beginning, you're mostly just making ends meet and breaking even. However, as you go along, you will discover that it gets better. You will just have to be patient and persevere. In some cases, you will find that you have two work seasons, "feast and famine," and you'll have to become accustomed to living life on the edge for a little while.

You Have an Excellent Network of People Who Can Help Bring the Idea to Fruition

Do you remember the different people you should have on your contact list? Coaches, connectors, mentors, and other acquaintances, for example? You need to have an active list of people who can vouch for you if times get rough. It's important to also have people who believe in you and can support you through the transition. It is hard at the beginning and having a group of people who have your back is a crucial aspect of the process. This network of people can also bring you into contact with people who would be in need of your goods or services. You will need to market yourself and your brand, and with the help and advice of others who are in your field, you will find ways to capitalize on their knowledge. Then, you will become more profitable and productive. You often need to know more people so you can accomplish your goals. Find your network, nourish it by staying in touch with others, and support others with just as much passion and zeal. You will find that it can be a very meaningful experience.

WHEN TO STOP THE JOB SEARCH AND START PLANNING THE LAUNCH OF YOUR OWN BUSINESS

There are some signs you need to watch out for the right time to start your own business. Heed them with caution and then proceed to your next business venture.

You Realize That You've Become Way Too Independent to Work for Someone Else Again

You probably want to be your own man or woman. You have an ideal future that you are planning for, and you want to get ready for each step of the process. With your business plan, budget, and financial plan on hand, you are ready to make a difference in the world by creating your own brand. There is a distinctive style that markets you and your true talents and skills, and you want to share it with the entire world. The world is your oyster, and you're ready to make your big break. If you find yourself thinking this way, then you are probably ready to start your own business.

You Need Freedom and Flexibility That a Regular Job Cannot Offer

You need freedom and flexibility in your job. You cannot accomplish all the things that you want to do with your side hustle right now, so you have to make compromises. But if you are starting your business, you don't want to have one foot in and one foot out. You have to be all in, 100%. You need to be completely focused on your business to have the best shot at making it successful. That means spending a *full-time-job's* worth of time on your new business. You want to create your own life, and with this freedom and autonomy, you can work endlessly on promoting your goods and services, and on finding clients who will support you in the process.

You Know That You Have Nothing to Lose

When you want freedom and autonomy and you're all in, the whole world is at your fingertips. You can take this big risk, because you know that it comes with a promise of great things for your future. However, you also have a backup plan-- if all else fails, you will end up having to seek employment again. You would be back on the job market, which, with your contacts and your network, will not be the end of the world. Don't worry about that. Consider what you can do now to make your dreams come true. Keep your eye on the prize: it will help you climb mountains. Sometimes, we just need to scale the highest cliff before we realize our truest potential. Continue to look up to the sky and it will be your only limit.

You've Experimented with the Idea While Still Employed

One final sign that you should stop your job search and launch your own business instead is that you have experimented with the idea while you were still at your day job, and it yielded some good results. Maybe you had a successful side hustle and you were bringing in some extra cash easily and effortlessly; you also quickly gained a steady stream of good clients to keep you busy.

If you're finding success in your side job and it is easily giving you more than half of your salary, it might be a good idea to consider quitting your current job in the near future. You might find that you will be profitable quickly, and have more free time by making your side job your main income source.

Especially if you are finding good clients who keep coming back to you and give you a ton of work, you might want to look into starting your business as soon as you can. It will be all worth it in the end.

SIGNS THAT YOU'RE NOT READY TO START YOUR OWN BUSINESS YET

You Like the Idea of Having Your Own Business, Not the Work You'll Have to Put in It

You may be dreaming of success as an entrepreneur.

But don't get all starry eyed and think that the process of starting your own business is going to be easy. It's definitely going to be a challenge. Although you might have visions of raking in money and think of becoming a millionaire within a year or two, don't get too disappointed, but it is probably not going to happen. Think of working on a startup project as a process; it's not a destination. Every part of the process matters, so you have to do all you can to ensure that you don't fall into the trap of thinking that it's going to be easy work, because no-- that's not just going to happen. Hard work and dedication are required if you want to see your business succeed, and often, you will have to commit heart and soul to it, through all circumstances (Schenecker, n.d.).

You Don't Have an Original Product or Service

You have to compete in order to succeed. You have to be the best at your craft in order to be respected by others. However, you need to be working toward creating something new and not merely using something that another person has created for you. Instead, you have to create your own brand and market your own product, something that is completely original to you. You should also be the one who is the sole provider of that good or service so that no one can compete with you and you become the gold standard.

It's important for you to keep your ideas fresh and original, so you can compete on the global market and successfully promote your business (Schenecker, n.d.).

You're Terrified of Failure

When you start something, you should be curious about all that is involved. With curiosity as your guide, you will find that failure doesn't exist, because you don't have any concrete goals. Instead, you discover what interests the customers, what product can attract them, and how you can give your best to them for your business. Through the entire learning process, you become successful. If you start becoming fearful about what will happen, then you will stop being brave and taking the necessary risks to start a business. When you stop trying, then you are truly failing.

It is possible you might be a perfectionist. It is best to fail early in this case. When you start your own business, the work is never complete. A startup never stays the same as it was in the beginning. It evolves and develops, so you need to be prepared to take action or change course. Not everything is going to be perfect. There will likely be kinks here and there that you will have to work on, but that's totally normal, and you should expect to encounter these rocks on the trail. However, if you get too concerned with failing in the beginning, your business will not be able to take off and scale the heights that you've always imagined it would.

As you go about creating this new business, you will find that there will be exhausting lessons you will have to learn. Working on a startup is going to test and train you like no other thing. Your passion and patience will be tested to the max, your attitude toward everything, from money, to creativity, self-worth, and the value you bring to your goods or service will be evaluated constantly. Therefore, you need to adopt a "can-do" mindset that is willing to learn from every scenario that you experience (Schenecker, n.d.).

Money Management Is a Problem

Perhaps, you have not been able to stick to a budget for a long time and you're buried in credit card or other debt. If this is the case, then you absolutely should not consider quitting your job and starting a business. Money management is one of the most important parts of having a successful startup; if you're struggling to make ends meet or pay the bills, it might be best for you to first learn budgeting skills, work on your savings, and then consider starting your own business.

You're Considering Quick Profit Opportunities, Not Something That Will Keep on Delivering in the Long Run

Moreover, if you want to make a profit, be aware that it

may actually take years for you to see any profit from your business. According to Small Business Trends, only 40% of startups are able to make significant profits on their business, with 82% of small business failures being directly linked to cash-flow difficulties (McCamy, 2019). It's going to take a long time, at least a few years, before your business is going to be able to pay you a living wage. If you put too much pressure on your business from the start, it is going to struggle to survive (McCamy, 2019). You might also live in a constant state of anxiety and depression, which is certainly not going to help with the success of your business.

Stick to your business plan for specific goals for the future, and then you will be able to know what you need to do to succeed. You can also project how far you will go with your profits in the future. Be realistic on this: do not expect miracles to happen overnight, and don't expect to build a successful startup overnight. It will take time, patience and hardwork, and you need to plan accordingly.

You're Not Aware of the Financials, Measuring Success and Strategically Planning for the Future

You might also be unaware of the financial aspects of starting your own business, including bench markers for your own success, and marketing plans that will ensure the success of your venture. You definitely need to have a roadmap in place, which can be used as a guide for every decision you make. No more making hasty and unplanned responses to things: instead, you need to be meticulous and proactive in the process of getting your business off the ground. Prepare financially for all aspects of your venture: that includes office space, supplies, human resources, marketing strategies, equipment, and anything else that requires a financial investment. In many cases, startups require a lot of initial costs, and it will always be more than you expect. Therefore, the more you are prepared, the more likely you will be able to get your business off the ground quickly.

While You're Curious About the Idea, You Don't Have a Business Plan

It is vital for a small-business owner to manage his or her finances well. If you're not watching your money, then you might need to make adjustments to your overall plan. And with a good business plan, you can improve your new startup's chances of survival. Moreover, you need to create a business plan to manage all aspects of actually starting and developing your business, including all the goals that you want to pursue in your work. Stick with your gut on this, and work hard to try to achieve everything you set your mind to, because as you continually reach higher, and realistically implement your plan following the guidelines you set for yourself, you will be able to add on to your business plan to achieve even more in the future.

SUMMARY

As you can see, there are a lot of things to consider when starting your own business. It's not a simple process, and you have to really take it one step at a time. And if you're not ready for it, then don't go for it until you are fully ready, both financially and mentally. There is nothing worse than starting your own business, only to have all your dreams and goals go down the drain because of poor planning and money management problems, which would undoubtedly cause your business to collapse. However, you shouldn't be afraid of failure, because a failure to start is a bigger failure, one that is going to stop you from chasing your dreams for a long time.

If you are in a positive position financially, and armed with an excellent business plan, then you might be well on your way to starting your own business. And you should go for it, because only time will tell if you will be able to succeed. You just have to jump in and get things rolling. It won't be easy. Don't expect instantaneous or even quick results. But once you start moving, you will find that it becomes easier and more natural the more time, skills and expertise you invest in your business venture. Weigh the costs and carefully consider whether you're prepared, and then get ready for battle, then get out there and prepare to make your world debut. It will be worth it.

CONCLUSION

No one wants to feel like they are stuck and unable to move from their current job. It is an uncomfortable place to be. When you start to feel the need to complain, stop yourself, and take action instead. This book has been about reflecting, researching, and taking action for your career and your advancement in the professional world.

In *Own Your Career*, we have challenged you to *"unstuck yourself"* from the difficult situations that you may face. Perhaps, you have held on to a job that is not offering you an opportunity for professional growth. Your pay is not increasing from year to year, but your responsibilities keep growing. Although you may not realize that you have options, you can research and re-design your career. Through a process of introspection, reflection, and discovery, you can find the career you were meant to have all along. And by having a support system and a professional network, the possibilities available to you will be endless.

It is difficult to make a move. All of our instincts tell us to stay in a comfortable place. Whenever we feel secure and safe, we don't want to move. We feel the need to stay put, because as humans we are naturally resistant to change. But you shouldn't stay in a situation where you will stagnate and not get better at what you do. You always have to be learning something new, in whatever situation you find yourself. By constantly improving your career, you will grow and see the potential for a successful and prosperous professional life.

Whether you are looking to climb the corporate ladder and get the job of your dreams, or you dream of opening your own business and trying your hand at freelancing and entrepreneurship, you can achieve your goals and dreams. You just have to want it bad enough, and you have to go after it with your whole heart. In the professional world, you cannot go at it halfheart-edly. You're either all in or all out. Find a way to ignite your passion and go for a career that is going to be meaningful, profitable, and secure. You can "unstuck yourself" and go where you need to be.

Thank you for joining us as we have shown you the

secrets to successfully change your career. Believe in yourself. You can do it. Don't settle for anything less than what you're worth. Climb the ladder and go where you have always wanted to go. You will be happier and more satisfied, just the way you were always meant to be.

AFTERWORD

Are you ready to pursue the career of your dreams? Don't just sit there on your couch with your computer in tow. Get ready to nail that interview and "kick ass!" With the tips, illustrations, and guides that we have presented in this book, you will be prepared to own your career to make a better you. You have gotten this far. Don't stop here. Keep going and head toward your goals.

With every successful job candidate is a goal and dream, a vision of the future. You have to have a motivation and center that is your *raison-d'etre* in the job market. Without it, your career will be directionless. Find your sense of direction, your personal compass, which will enable you to successfully find the job you were meant to have all along.

The information in this book is based on real-life experiences with real people, who have made their dreams possible. Feeling inspired and ready to go? Using this info, you will be on your way to finding your calling in a career. Maybe you're looking to climb the career ladder or want to get a promotion at your job. If you follow our trusted advice, you will most certainly be successful.

The world today has grown more competitive than ever before. The best positions are up for grabs, and you need to be ready to stand out with a shiny, polished CV that will impress and attract companies to you.

Owning your career is your responsibility, no one else is going to do it for you. You must be the self-reliant, productive, and ambitious career professional you were meant to be. Live it. Become a confident person who protrudes warmth, personality, and charisma and you will find yourself in a career that greatly rewards your purposeful ambition. I hope this book has helped you see that and will lead you to where you want to be.

Thank you for choosing this book. May it lead you to success and prosperity, as you pursue your unique and fabulous career path. It's going to be exciting, and you will become a more innovative and beautiful person inside and out. I'm rooting for you; you can do it!

REFERENCES

THE CAREER OF CONSEQUENCE: FINDING WHAT SERVES YOU

Achor, Shawn (2011). *The Happy Secret to Better Work.* [Video File] TED Talk. Retrieved from https://www.ted.com/talks/shawn_achor_the_happy_secret_to_better_work?language=en

Big Think Edge (2018). "Top 8 Interpersonal Skills for the Workplace." *Big Think Edge.* [online] Retrieved from https://www.bigthinkedge.com/top-8-interpersonal-skills-for-the-workplace/

Caprino, Kathy (2013). "7 Essentials For A Happy and Fulfilling Career." Forbes Magazine. [online] Retrieved from https://www.forbes.com/sites/kathycaprino/

2013/08/26/7-essentials-for-a-happy-and-fulfilling-career/#251157fe1c1d

Clark Kegley-Refusing to Settle (2016, December 22). *How to Find Your Life's Purpose In Under 10 Minutes.* [Video File] Youtube. Retrieved from https://www.youtube.com/watch?v=VnhQvqtJKeU

The Corporate Ladder: Definition, Structure, and Positions (n.d.). Study.com. [online] Retrieved from https://study.com/academy/lesson/the-corporate-ladder-definition-structure-positions.html

EF (n.d.). 11 Tips For How to Ace a Job Interview. EF [blog] Retrieved from https://www.ef.com/wwen/blog/language/11-tips-how-to-ace-a-job-interview/

Gerke, Natalie (2015). "83% of Millennials – Now Largest Group of New Parents — Would Leave Their Job for One with Better Family/Lifestyle Benefits." Market Watch. [online] Retrieved from https://www.marketwatch.com/press-release/83-of-millennials-now-largest-group-of-new-parents-would-leave-their-job-for-one-with-better-familylifestyle-benefits-2015-08-12

Kagan, Julia (2019). "Networking-Definition." *Investopedia.* [online] Retrieved from https://www.investopedia.com/terms/n/networking.asp

Kenton, Will (2019). "Social Capital-Definition." *Investopedia*. [online] Retrieved from https://www. investopedia.com/terms/s/socialcapital.asp

Lebowitz, Shana (2018). 21 Psychological Tricks That Will Help You Ace a Job Interview. Ladders- the $100K Club. [online] Retrieved from https://www.theladders. com/career-advice/21-psychological-tricks-that-will-help-you-ace-a-job-interview

Lexico (n.d.). "Career- Definition." *Lexico: Powered by Oxford*. Retrieved from https://www.lexico.com/en/ definition/career

Murphy, Nikelle (2017). "How to Look for a New Job While You Still Have Your Old One." *ShowBiz Cheat-Sheet*. [online] Retrieved from https://www.cheatsheet. com/money-career/how-to-look-for-a-new-job-while-you-still-have-your-old-one.html/

Perception Trainers (2014). "5 Tools For Finding Your Purpose in Life." *Weekly Perspective*. Retrieved from https://perceptiontrainers.com/5-tools-for-finding-your-purpose-in-life/

Phillpott, Sion (2019). "The Importance of Interpersonal Skills in the Workplace." *Career Addict*. [online] Retrieved from https://www.careeraddict.com/the-importance-of-interpersonal-skills-in-the-workplace

Rasmussen, Dawn (2016). "5 Secrets of Climbing the Career Ladder." *Work It Daily.* Retrieved from https://www.workitdaily.com/secrets-climbing-career-ladder

Sciortino, Tricia (2019). "7 Tips to Help Millennials Climb the Corporate Ladder." *The Balance Careers.* [online] Retrieved from https://www.thebalancecareers.com/millennials-climb-corporate-ladder-1918060

Smith, Jacquelyn (2013). "The 13 Dos and Don'ts of Job Searching While You're Still Employed." Forbes Magazine. [online] Retrieved from https://www.forbes.com/sites/jacquelynsmith/2013/10/29/the-13-dos-and-donts-of-job-searching-while-youre-still-employed/#4c834d42c405

Smith, Jeremey Adam (2018). "How to Find Your Purpose in Life." *Greater Good Magazine: Berkeley.* [online] Retrieved from https://greatergood.berkeley.edu/article/item/how_to_find_your_purpose_in_life

Vojinovic, Ivana (2019). "Job Satisfaction Statistics: Keep Your Workers Happy and Your Business Healthy." *Small Biz Genius.* [online] Retrieved from https://www.smallbizgenius.net/by-the-numbers/job-satisfaction-statistics/

Whitehorn, Katherine (n.d.). Wikiquotes. [online]

Retrieved from https://en.wikiquote.org/ wiki/Katharine_Whitehorn

Young, Jeffrey (2017). "How Many Times Will People Change Jobs? The Myth of the Endlessly-Job-Hopping Millennial." EdSurge. [online] Retrieved from https:// www.edsurge.com/news/2017-07-20-how-many- times-will-people-change-jobs-the-myth-of-the- endlessly-job-hopping-millennial

UNSTUCK YOURSELF

11+ Career Action Plan Examples – PDF, Word. Examples.- com. https://www.examples.com/business/career- action-plan.html

Adkins, A. (n.d.). *Millennials: The Job-Hopping Generation.* Gallup. https://www.gallup.com/workplace/231587/ millennials-job-hopping-generation.aspx

Alini, E. (2018, January 8). *Why you should switch jobs every 2 to 3 years to boost your earnings.* Global News. https://globalnews.ca/news/3946085/switching-jobs- pay-boost/

Autenrieth, N. (n.d.). *10 Tips on Effectively Looking for a Job While Employed.* Top Resume. https://www. topresume.com/career-advice/10-tips-on-effectively- looking-for-a-job-while-employed

Ceniza-Levine, C. (2018). *Networking For A Career Change -- Seven Contacts To Prioritize.* Forbes. https://www.forbes.com/sites/carolinecenizalevine/2018/04/15/networking-for-a-career-change-seven-contacts-to-prioritize/#7fee1f7c126b

Ceniza-Levine, C. (2018). *When Is It Okay To Quit Your Job Without Another Job Lined Up? A Ten-Question Checklist.* Forbes. https://www.forbes.com/sites/carolinecenizalevine/2018/08/18/when-is-it-okay-to-quit-your-job-without-another-job-lined-up-a-ten-question-checklist/#1a715eec4e90

Ferguson, N. (2018). *Career Changers! Here are Six Actionable Steps to Help You Land a Job in a New Role or Industry.* LinkedIn.https://www.linkedin.com/pulse/6-actionable-steps-help-you-land-job-new-role-natasha-ferguson

Huddleston, C. (2019, April 28). *Quitting Without Another Job? Here Are 16 Tips From People Who've Taken the Big Leap.* Yahoo! Finance. https://finance.yahoo.com/news/quitting-without-another-job-16-090000799.html

Keng, C. (2014). *Employees Who Stay In Companies Longer Than Two Years Get Paid 50% Less.* Forbes. https://www.forbes.com/sites/cameronkeng/2014/06/22/employees-that-stay-in-companies-longer-than-2-

years-get-paid-50-less/#77628fa6e07f

Lande, S. (n.d.). *Why a Career Change May Make You Happier (and How to Successfully Make the Leap)*. The Muse. https://www.themuse.com/advice/why-a-career-change-may-make-you-happier

Liu, J. (2019, September 7). *The 10 fastest-growing jobs of the next decade—and what they pay*. CNBC. https://www.cnbc.com/2019/09/07/these-are-the-10-fastest-growing-jobs-of-the-next-decade.html

McCamy, L. (2019, January 2). *8 signs you're not ready to start your own business*. Business Insider. https://www.businessinsider.com/signs-not-ready-to-start-your-own-business-2018-11#7-youre-not-willing-to-go-out-and-market-your-idea-7

McKay, D. (2019). *How to Make a Career Choice When You Are Undecided*. The Balance Careers. https://www.thebalancecareers.com/steps-to-choosing-career-525506

Monster (n.d.). *Your professional networking questions – answered*. Monster.com. https://www.monster.co.uk/career-advice/article/what-is-networking-and-how-do-i-do-it

Nemko, M. (2015). *Overcoming Fear of Looking for a Job*. Psychology Today. https://www.psychologytoday.com/

us/blog/how-do-life/201503/overcoming-fear-looking-job

Occupational Outlook Handbook for Social Workers. (2019, September 4). *U.S. Bureau of Labor Statistics.* https://www.bls.gov/ooh/community-and-social-service/social-workers.htm

Power, R. (n.d.). *23 Percent of Workers Regret Switching Jobs: Here's How to Make the Right Move.* Inc. https://www.inc.com/rhett-power/23-percent-of-workers-regret-switching-jobs-heres-how-to-make-right-move.html

Schenecker, B. (n.d.). *7 Reasons You're Not Ready to Start Your Own Business.* Business Collective. https://businesscollective.com/7-reasons-youre-not-ready-to-start-your-own-business/index.html

Stanley, N. (2015). *What To Do When You're Scared Of Making A Change – And Of Staying Where You Are.* Careershifters. https://www.careershifters.org/expert-advice/what-to-do-when-youre-scared-of-making-a-change-and-of-staying-where-you-are

Tell Truth Quotes (n.d.). Goodreads. https://www.goodreads.com/quotes/tag/tell-truth

U.S. Bureau of Labor Statistics (2019). Economic News Release: Employment Projections: 2018-2028

Summary. Bls.gov. https://www.bls.gov/news.release/ecopro.nr0.htm

Victoria State Government Education and Training (n.d.) *Career Action Plan Templates*. State Government of Victoria, Australia. https://www.education.vic.gov.au/school/teachers/teachingresources/careers/carframe/Pages/cap.aspx

Zhang, L. (n.d.). *5 Smart Networking Strategies for Career Changers*. The Muse. https://www.themuse.com/advice/5-smart-networking-strategies-for-career-changers

Printed in Great Britain
by Amazon